Sir James K

1855 – 1934

Tyneside's most charitable

shipowner

Mike N. Coates

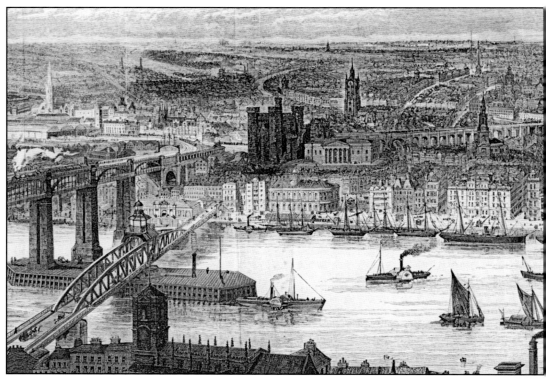

Newcastle quayside at a time when Sir James Knott had his office here.

The front cover shows the mouth of the River Tyne with Knott's Flats

towering over it on the north bankside

Copyright Mike N. Coates 2023

ISBN : 978 - 1 - 3999 - 6334 - 3

This book has been printed with the generous support of the Sir James Knott Trust

Contents

Preface

I was born in North Shields and when a child, could see from my house the flats towering over the river mouth which we knew as Knotts Flats. Not until sixty five years later when I became a volunteer and member of the research team at the Old Low Light Heritage Centre at North Shields Fish Quay, did I discover that many influential North Shields citizens, who had been born in North Shields, whose names can still be seen on buildings or street names had improved the lives of Shields folks.

Early in 2023 I wrote and published a book entitled "Inspirational North Shields Folks" about the life stories of eight of these people who I had researched for talks and exhibitions we had presented at the Old Low Light Heritage Centre. Amongst these, in my opinion Sir James Knott was to me, the most inspirational and justified this separate book. His entrepreneurial skills and success in the shipping trade combined with his philanthropic nature enabled him to create a charity which almost 100 years after his death, still improves the lives of so many people in our area and after whom these flats were named.

As a young man, like Sir James, I worked in a shipping office in Newcastle. My father had spent his entire working life on Newcastle quayside working for another shipping company and my grandfather also worked on the river for the River Improvement Commissioners. My next door neighbour worked for yet another shipping company as at this time so many people living on Tyneside were employed in shipping, either in ship building, repairing, crewing or supplying what was then a massive industry. So the River Tyne touched and supported so many families.

When researching family or local history we find so many connections to the past. I attended Salem Methodist Church with my parents and grandparents and I have now discovered my great grandfather and Sir James, who were the same age, both attended this church at the same time so would have known each other. In my first few years I lived in Alma Place, a few doors down from where Sir James had lived and for a while I lived in Cullercoats, a few doors along the street from where Sir James had lived in Monks Haven 80 years earlier.

Realising we have looked at the same views, possibly entered the same buildings and walked the same streets as these inspirational local people means all these connections however tenuous, link us to the past which makes historical research so fascinating.

There have been many accounts written previously about Sir James Knott concentrating on his shipping fleet and business acumen, however in this book I have endeavoured to illustrate his benevolent nature and his role of devoted husband and father.

Mike Coates

1   Knott family and James' early life

The Sir James Knott Memorial Flats at Tynemouth are an imposing landmark at the entrance to the River Tyne and stand as a lasting memorial to one of Tyneside's most successful businessmen, Sir James Knott. They were built in the 1930s with money largely provided by the Knott Trust which had been formed to administer the large fortune amassed during his lifetime.

So who was Sir James Knott? The Knott family had moved from Hexhamshire in the late 1700s to Howdon, on the north bank of the River Tyne where his great-great-grandfather John and his eldest son John worked in Howdon Ropeworks. His second son Matthew (great-grandfather) was a shipwright and married Ann Miller on 8 November 1803 at St. Peter's Church, Wallsend and their second son, James (grandfather) born on 1 August 1807 married Mary Turnbull on 16 January 1828 at St. Nicholas Church, Newcastle (now the cathedral). Their eldest son Matthew, born in 1830, was Sir James' father.

This was a period when North Shields was booming with shipbuilding, fishing and the export of coal. After years of being repressed by Newcastle's strangle hold on trade on the Tyne, in 1803 the right to hold a market was granted, then with the building of a Customs House at North Shields in 1848, North and South Shields together were constituted as an independent port from Newcastle.

Sir James' parents, Matthew and Margaret Dobson, a butcher's daughter who was an assistant cook for a Newcastle merchant living on Westgate Road, were married on 6 June 1852 at St.Andrew's Church, Newcastle. They lived in Stephenson Street, Howdon where his father Matthew had set up in business as a ships biscuit maker, grocer and ship's chandler. Their first child Mary was born there in April 1853, then James on 31 January 1855. James, named after his grandfather, a master of collier brigs. is recorded as being baptised in the parish of Wallsend on 4 March 1855 with his father Matthew recorded as a blacksmith.

Then in October 1856, the family moved to North Shields and are listed on the 1861 Census residing at 49 Linskill Street. This was, as were all the streets in the area, Tyneside terraced flats where James' parents and the five children they had at the time, lived in three rooms with a toilet in the back yard. (These streets were demolished in the 1960s when the area was redeveloped with modern housing.)

Soon after, his father, Matthew, after eight years as a customs officer, in 1864, became the inn keeper of the Old Inn, Nile Street, North Shields and after a few years he changed the business to wine and spirit merchants operating from 52, 53, 54 Nile Street. On the 1871 Census Matthew and Margaret were living at 52 Nile Street with James and three of his brothers and two sisters. By 1877 Matthew had moved to 5 Lovaine Place, where he lived until he died on 24 April 1896 aged 66 years and was well known and highly respected. The Shields Daily News reported that through his indefatigable exertions and thorough business tact, he made himself a large trade having to extend his premises more than once. His cortege, which consisted of a hearse and nine carriages, left his home at one o'clock and he was interred in Preston Cemetery. Probate stated his estate was worth £3,454. 14s. 4d which equates to £320,000 today. James' mother, Margaret died at 5 Lovaine Place on 28 December 1899 aged 67 years and is also buried in nearby Preston Cemetery with Matthew and their children George and three Margarets who all died in childhood.

Altogether James had five brothers, Henry, George Turnbull (who died aged 10), Matthew, Stanley (who went to South Africa) and Herbert and 5 sisters Mary who was two years older than James, Annie Dobson, then three Margarets who died aged 2, 1 and 8. On the 1861 Census at 49 Linskill Street are listed Matthew (father aged 31), Margaret (mother aged 29), children Mary aged 8, James aged 6, Henry aged 4, George aged 2 and Margaret aged 3 months.

Parish [or Township] of	City or Municipal Borough of	HOUSES	Name and Surname of each Person	Relation to Head of Family	Condition	Age of		Rank, Profession, or Occupation	Where Born	

The Best Place for Wines & Spirits

M. KNOTT, WINE MERCHANT 52. 53. 54

M. KNOTT,

Nile Street, North Shields.

Rare Old Wines, Fine Old Matured Whiskies,
Brandies, Champagnes, Liqueurs, &c.

Matthew and Margaret's children were :-

Mary, their first child was born on 4 April 1853. On the 1871 Census aged 18 she was living at 69 Linskill Terrace married to Joseph Walter Scott Brown aged 22, a ship broker. By the 1891 Census she is living with Joseph at 6 Waterloo Place, Tynemouth.

No.	When Born.	Name, if any.	Sex.	Name and Surname of Father.	Name and Maiden Surname of Mother.	Rank or Profession of Father.	Signature, Description, and Residence of Informant.	When Registered.	Signature of Registrar.	Baptismal Name if added after Registration of Birth
258	Fourth April 1853 Willington Quay	Mary	Girl	Matthew Knott	Margaret Knott formerly Dobson	Grocer	Matthew Knott Father Willington Quay	Twenty seventh April 1853	Benjamin Forster Registrar	

Superintendent Registrar's District *Tynemouth*

Registrar's District *Wallsend*

1853. BIRTHS in the District of *Wallsend* in the County of *Northumberland*

Next was **James,** born 31 January 1855 at Willington Quay, baptised on 4 March at St Peters church, Wallsend.

Henry was next born on 24 May 1856 at North Shields. Henry followed his father in the wine business and married Francis K. Harrison of 83 Linskill Street (the same street where he lived) on 4 September 1881 and their oldest daughter Margaret married Sir James' son Thomas on 20 July 1925.

George Turnbull was next, born on 26 October 1858 and died aged 10 on 17 November 1868.

The first **Margaret** was born on 25 December 1860 and died aged 2 on 7 March 1863.

The family grave in North Shields cemetery

Then **Annie Dobson** born 24 November 1862, who married in 1886 aged 24 at Tynemouth, Alfred Josiah Baker also aged 24 from Maidstone, Kent who aged 19 on the 1881 Census was listed as a clerk in HM Customs boarding at 67 Howard Street. Presumably he came to Shields for work.

Matthew was the next born on 29 November 1864 who aged 16 was an articled clerk and by 1888 was a junior solicitor working at 21 Howard Street. On 6 February 1888 when living with his parents at 5 Lovaine Place he married Isabella Rogers Turpie at Morpeth who on the 1881 Census was living at 4 Frank Place listed aged 20, born in Morpeth. Also in 1881 Matthew's brother James was living at 1 Frank Place. A court case was recorded in the Shields Daily News of 19 May 1898 where Matthew accused the husband of his niece of badly physically assaulting him in the street after they had not spoken to each other for over a year since Matthew refused to lend him £5. Matthew won the case and the accused was fined 20s but the Bench refused Matthew his costs as they said his character was known to be not without question. Another court cast was reported in this newspaper on 11 August the same year when Matthew was charged in custody with having disobeyed an order of the Married Women's Maintenance Act to pay Mrs Knott £4.10s that had been due to her for six weeks. He pleaded he had not been in a position do pay this previously but would endeavour to borrow it from his mother. The court advised he would go to prison for a month if the money was not paid in the next two days.

On the 1901 Census Isabella, aged 39 is living as head of the house at 75 Chirton West View "living on own means" with her three children Grace aged 11, James aged 9 and Mildred aged 7. When Isabella died in July 1904 she was buried next to the Turpie family plot in North Shields cemetery. I can't find another reference to Matthew.

The second **Margaret** was born on 17 December 1866 and died on 12 January 1868 aged just one.

Then the third **Margaret** was christened on 20th November 1868 at Salem Methodist Church on Linskill Street, the street where the family lived at the time and died on 15 February 1876 aged eight.

The two youngest were **Stanley** born on 30 September 1870 and christened on 5 March 1871 also at Salem Methodist Church, and **Herbert** born 14 May 1872 and christened at Salem on 2 December 1872. They both appear on the 1881 Census, Stanley aged 10 and Herbert aged 8 at the East Keswick boarding school near Leeds. This was run by Joseph Laurenson as a preparatory theological college to train young men for the Methodist Ministry and missionary work overseas. Ten years later on the 1891 Census Herbert is back home at 5 Lovaine Place aged 18 listed as a fitter and draughtsman then on 12 October 1896 he marries at Cullercoats Wilhelmina Waddle who was born in 1875 and they live at Stanley House, Tynemouth. On the 1901 Census however, he is listed aged 30, married and a shopkeeper and hairdresser boarding at Kings Norton, Worcestershire but Wilhelmina is not recorded with him. She is on 1901 census aged 26 married, living on own means and boarding in Paddington, London. Herbert was still alive aged 52 in 1924 as his brother, then Sir James makes financial provisions for him. I cannot trace a record of his death.

Stanley who had the most adventurous life of their children may have agreed to be sent to Africa as a missionary for he is on the passenger list of the Hawarden Castle listed as a clerk returning to London on 2 June 1893 from Cape Town. He served for a year as a subaltern in the 6th Battalion Rifle Brigade then proceeded back to South Africa and enlisted in the Cape Mounted Police as a private and served in the Matabele War in 1896. When the Boer War broke out in 1899 he was Captain of Uitenhage Mounted Volunteers then in command of a company of Marshall's Horse Scouts for three years. He was mentioned in the Newcastle Courant of 23 December 1899 stating "Lieutenant Stanley Knott who had been in the Cape Mounted Police and had great experience in Rhodesia and the Cape, had now joined the Uitenhage Volunteers and left on 4 December for the front in the Boer War (Oct 1899 – May 1902).

He then must have returned to England as on 30 October 1908 he departs from Liverpool to New York on the White Star Steamer "Arabic" recorded on the passenger list as a clerk. On 10 June 1911 Census he is living in British Columbia, Canada aged 40, listed as a book keeper, giving his nationality as Canadian. On 16 November 1914 he enlists in the Canadian Overseas Expeditionary Force giving his brother James as his next of kin, military as his trade and stating he has previously served 18 years in a military force. He is a captain in the 29th Vancouver Battalion but resigns his commission just five months later as a casualty on 12 April 1915.

Less than a month later on the 7 May he arrives back in Liverpool having sailed from New York on the "Lapland" giving his occupation as rancher. He then enlisted with the Army Service Corps and was posted to France as recorded in the Newcastle Journal of 2 February

1918, stating Second Lieutenant Stanley Knott of the Army Service Corps, wounded in France after serving for three years, died suddenly at a camp in the south of England on 1 February and was buried in the Bungay Cemetery in Suffolk.

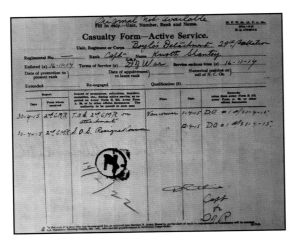

Sir James

It can be seen that he came from a fairly humble background, they were hard times with three of his sisters and a brother dying in childhood and one wonders what special attributes he possessed that made him so successful in business. As a boy he lived in Linskill Street, in a typical Tyneside terraced flat of the time of three rooms with a toilet in the back yard. He was educated at the school attached to the Scotch Church in Howard Street, a few streets away in North Shields.

Linskill Street   **Scotch Church**

He left school at the age of 14 to start work as a shipping clerk on Lombard Street on Newcastle Quayside with Borries Craig and Company, Merchants and Ship Brokers dealing mainly in timber. Arguably he could have chosen an easier path for his chosen profession and followed in his father's business, being the oldest son, as his younger brother Henry did but perhaps because of the influence of the teetotal preaching of the Methodist school and church he attended, he felt he couldn't encourage the use of alcohol.

It was reported in the Shields Hustler magazine that he was known in the town as a young enthusiastic gardener, cultivating his plot on the old allotments near Spring Gardens (these were at the top of Nile Street where he lived at the time) and as a worker in the Howard Street Wesleyan Sunday School. The garden and church were both formative influences which lasted throughout his life.

In April 1876 to gain more knowledge of the shipping business, he entered into a partnership with the Newcastle shipbroker firm of James Thompson and Company. Their office was on a chare leading down to the river called Burn Bank. The partnership now called, Thompson, Knott and Company was mainly with visiting sailing ships from Yorkshire, exporting coal to the near continent. This partnership lasting only three years until 1 June 1879 when James who at the age of 23 had realised ship owning offered him more opportunities. He borrowed the sum of £500 and launched his own business, part of which he used to purchase a 45 year old collier brig, his first ship, called the "Pearl of Scarborough" for £186. This was financed by a consortium of investors including his father and contacts he had made at the Newcastle Exchange during his time as a shipbroker. The Newcastle Exchange was where most of the commercial business was conducted, where shipowners, ship brokers and agents would meet. The Pearl was mainly used to carry coal from the Tyne to Rouen in northern France. This was at a time when the majority of people in Tyneside earned their living from the shipping trade in one form or another, actually manning ships, providing stores, building or repairing, management or dock work.

Model of the Brig "Pearl"

His next ship, a 32 year old brig, "Rival" was bought in November 1879 but was wrecked the next month. He wasn't much luckier with his third ship which was 35 years old and lasted no more than six months. He wasn't discouraged however and by 1881 he had done well enough in business to order from Swan Hunter's at Wallsend his first steam ship the 'Saxon Prince', which was 832 tons gross, 530 tons net, intended principally for coal and the Spanish ore trade and this was the first of the later world famous Prince Shipping Line. He had vision and was quick to see the possibilities of changing technical developments in the shipping industry, in particular the value of steam.

He owned up to over 20 collier brigs, all plying their trade along the east coast, managed from an office in Milburn House, Newcastle. It is said that in his private office here, there was a large chart of the seven seas into which he fitted small wooden models of his ships, mounted on pegs so he could follow their movements.

The Customs House on Newcastle Quayside where all new ships had to be registered was only a short walk from his office at Milburn House but he registered all his new steamers at the Customs House at North Shields, an indication of his pride in his home town.

Milburn House, Newcastle upon Tyne

Howard Street Wesleyan Church

Although James family attended Salem Methodist Church on Linskill Street where his family lived at the time he became a regular attendee and helper at Howard Street Wesleyan Church and there, on 17 September 1878, he married his first wife **Margaret Annie Garbutt** when they were both 24.

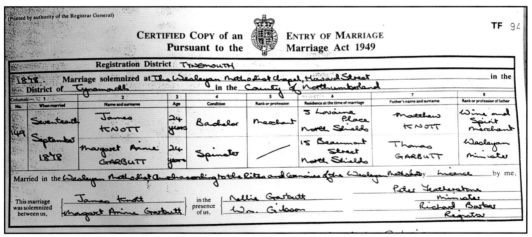

Margaret, born in Holmfirth in July 1854, was the daughter of the late Rev. Thomas Garbutt, the Wesleyan Methodist minister and his wife Margaret. In September 1860 Rev. Thomas Garbutt was appointed Superintendent of the South Shields Wesleyan Circuit and took up residence in Winterbottom Street, Westoe, South Shields but after only three weeks there he felt poorly on a Saturday evening. A doctor attended him on the following Tuesday, diagnosed Scarlet Fever and he died that evening aged only 46. As James was only five years old at the time he obviously did not know his future father in law yet later named his first son after him.

Salem Church in mid 1960s   **Article in Durham Chronicle 28 September 1860**

On the 1861 Census, Margaret was living with her mother, sister and two brothers at Winterbottom Street but by the 1871 Census was a pupil aged 17 at Savil Park School, Halifax. Sometime after this the family moved to North Shields as on her wedding certificate her address was shown as 15 Beaumont Street, which is just a street away from Nile Street where James lived and they both lived just a few minutes' walk from their Wesleyan Church in Howard Street.

It may be that because of the teachings of the Wesleyan Church or perhaps from Margaret's influence that James didn't follow in his father's business "the demon drink" and James appears to have been teetotal. In 1885 when the annual Temperance Conference was held at Brunswick Place Chapel in Newcastle, he chartered a Tyne ferry to take the ministers and friends from the meeting on a trip down the River Tyne to St. Mary's Island and back and provided lunch for them on board. Later in the rule booklet for the Knott Trust it stated that requests for grants were to be given priority if the applicants did not have alcohol on their premises.

When first married James and Margaret lived at 6 Frank Place where Thomas Garbutt Knott was born on 14 July 1879 and in 1881 they moved to 1 Frank Place where James Leadbitter Knott was born 2 December 1882. On the same Census at number 2 is his mother in law Margaret Garbutt, aged 55, listed as head of household and an annuitant. At number 4 is Isabella Turpie who later marries Matthew junior. They appeared to be a very close family. Then in 1887 James and his family moved just round the corner to the more substantial 4 Alma Place.

Frank Place

The undermentioned Houses are situate within the Boundaries of the

Civil Parish [or Township] of	City or Municipal Borough of	Municipal Ward of	Parliamentary Borough of	Town or Village or Hamlet of	Urban Sanitary District of	Rural Sanitary District of	Ecclesiastical Parish or District of
Preston	Tynemouth	North Shields	Tynemouth		Tynemouth		Tynemouth

No. of Schedule	ROAD, STREET, &c., and No. or NAME of HOUSE	HOUSES Inhabited (U.), or (B.)	NAME and Surname of each Person	RELATION to Head of Family	CONDITION as to Marriage	AGE last Birthday of Males	Females	Rank, Profession, or OCCUPATION	WHERE BORN	If (1) Deaf-and-Dumb (2) Blind (3) Imbecile or Idiot (4) Lunatic
78	Preston Lane		Constance Fryack	daur			10	Scholar	North'd North Shields	
79	1 Frank Pl.	1	James Knott	Head	Mar	24		Ship Broker	Yorkshire Howdon	
			Margaret do	Wife	Mar		26		Yorkshire Homeforth	
			Thomas G. do	Son		1			North'd North Shields	
			Ester Gray	Serv	Unm		28	General Servant	North'd Seghill	
80	2 do do	1	Margaret Garbutt	Head	W		53	Annuitant	Norfolk Upper Sheringham	
			Elenor J. do	daur	Unm		28		Yorkshire Whitby	
			Charles H. do	Son	Mar	24		Jobbing Watchmaker	North'd North Shields	
			Bethie do	daur in Law	Mar		23		Bedfordshire Bedford	
81	3 do do	1	Sarah A. Harlam	Head	W		44		North'd North do	
			William do	Son	Unm	16		Apprentice (F.)	do do	
			Sarah do	Dau			13	Scholar	do do	
			Margaret do	Dau			12	do	do do	
			Thomas do	Son		9		do	do do	
			Agnes do	Dau			6		do do	
			Amy D. do	Dau			2		do do	
			Robetta Grant	Serv	Unm		18	General Servant	do do	
82	4 do do	1	Isabella M. Turpie	Head	Unm		20		do do	
			Andrew J. do	Brother		17		Clerk	do do	
			Mary J. Hewson	Serv	Unm		20	General Servant	do Howdon	
83	5 do do	1	William Knott	Head	Mar	58		Master Butcher	Durham Hebson	
			Sarah do	Wife	Mar		47		Durham Hebson	
			James Cromarty	Brother in law	Mar	54		Ship-wright	Stromness	
			Elizabeth do	Sister in law	Mar		56		Durham Hebron	
			Ann do	Visitor	Mar		52		do do	
5	Total of Houses...	5			Total of Males and Females...	8	14			

NOTE.—Draw the pen through such of the words of the headings as are inappropriate.

1881 Census for Frank Place

Alma Place

2   The start of his shipping empire

The Prince Steam Shipping Company Ltd was formed in 1883 with the white Prince of Wales feathers adopted as the company crest. Further steamships were ordered and the first of these commenced trading in 1884. By 1886 the company's fleet comprised 20 sailing ships and 17 ocean-going steamships. Between 1882 and 1887 nine sailing vessels were lost in bad weather and if the wind was unfavourable these ships couldn't leave or enter port. Realising the advantage and manoeuvrability of steam propulsion a year later the sailing vessels were sold and Knott applied himself to the development of a fleet of steamships engaged in world-wide trade. Part of his success was attributed to his ability to recognise a business opportunity, by acquiring vessels that their original owner no longer required, by purchasing second hand vessels at favourable costs and indeed many of his vessels were second hand. When James studied Law in London from June 1885 until January 1889, William Milburn his right hand man, managed his business on Tyneside and in 1887 when James disposed of his fleet of sailing vessels, Milburn bought 16 of them. James Milburn was also a director of the North Shields fishing company Richard Irvin and Sons and maintained a fleet of second hand sailing vessels. In the next two years six new steamers were registered, four coming from Short Brothers of Sunderland which began a close relationship between owner and builder resulting in Sir James owning 37 steamers built by Shorts. This was in the days before competitive tendering and repeat orders would be placed by a satisfied customer. Among the earliest services advertised were those between the UK and Tripoli, Malta, Tunis, Egypt, Cyprus, Palestine and Syria.

How Newcastle Quayside looked when James Knott had his offices here

In 1887 Charles Parsons after experimenting with a steam turbine engine in his yacht "Turbinia" purchased the "Eastern Prince" from Knott to develop the engine further in order to later sell them to shipowners such as James Knott. Parsons removed the machinery and installed new geared turbine machinery to increase efficiency, which was a success but James Knott did not use it in any of his ships. They were associates and after Charles Parsons was President of the Institute of Marine Engineers in 1906, James Knott became President in

1908, a great honour for a ship owner. After Sir James moved to Close House, they became neighbours with Parsons living at Holeyn Hall, Wylam less than two miles away from the Knotts.

By 1888 the company was firmly established on routes from Europe and New York to Brazil and the River Plate and in the years leading up to the First World War, it carried one third of the total coffee crop from Brazil to New York and New Orleans. With the opening of the Manchester Ship Canal in 1894, a service was instituted between Manchester and Alexandria for the importation of Egyptian cotton. Manufactured goods and machinery were exported through Manchester. In 1895 he set up the Prince Line Ltd, which he went on to build up to be the third largest privately owned shipping line in the world with 45 ships, many of them built in Tyne and Wear shipyards, primarily by Short Bros. The ships had slate grey hulls, black and red funnels with white Prince of Wales feathers and to promote the line he paid his sailors extra for wearing the company jersey with "Prince Line" in white across the chest and cap ribbons bearing the ship's name.

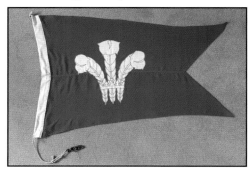 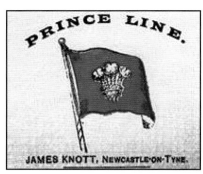

In 1897 he formed the Prince Steam Shipping Association which absorbed the entire range of Knott's shipping interests, principally the Prince Steam Shipping Company Ltd and the Prince Steam shipping Insurance Association, founded in 1887. As older ships were replaced by new and larger tonnage, a regular line was built on the carriage of Italian emigrants to New York and a regular fortnightly service between New York and the Mediterranean. In the early years of the 20th century a service from New York to South Africa, India and the Far East was inaugurated. By 1900 he had a fleet of 38 vessels and was trading all over the world. This increased to 45 vessels by 1914. The service from the Tyne to Central America, Mexico and New Orleans carrying coal and coke was the most favoured by the Geordie seamen who manned the ships since it allowed them to embark and disembark at their home port. In the year before the declaration of war four steamers joined the fleet from Sunderland yards, two of which were lost in the war and these were the last vessels completed for the Prince Line to the order of Sir James.

Saxon Prince (2)

Saxon Prince (1) was built in 1882 by C. S. Swan & Hunter at Newcastle with a tonnage of 832grt, a length of 215ft, a beam of 30ft 8in and a service speed of 9 knots. Registered at North Shields she was James Knott's first steamship. On 20 October 1914 she was stopped and scuttled by U-17 when 14 miles off Norway. She was supposedly the first merchant ship sunk by a submarine in World War 1.   Saxon Prince (2) was built in 1899 by Short Bros. at Sunderland with a tonnage of 3471grt, a length of 352ft 7in, a beam of 45ft 7in and a service speed of 10 knots. Built for Prince Line Ltd she entered service in July 1899. On 25 February 1916 she was captured by the German auxiliary cruiser Mowe 620 miles west of Fastnet and sunk with explosives.

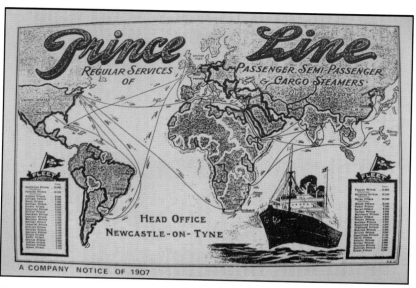

A COMPANY NOTICE OF 1907

Syrian Prince 1893

Royal Prince 1907

Throughout the time that he was in the shipping business, Sir James had 32 ships built in Tyne and Wear shipyards, primarily by Short Bros. He expected the same commitment from his ship's officers to hard work as he possessed and all the ships carried the following warning inscribed on their bridges:

All accidents are the Result of Carelessnes

And indeed if any of his ships were involved in an accident, all of its officers were compelled to resign.

It was well known that Sir James believed that the Prince ships and crew should benefit from the best conditions possible. He referred to this principle at the shareholders annual meeting in 1913 when he said "looking back on 40 years of sailing and steamship ownership and management, I realise as a general principle that it is in the interest of shareholders, managers and employees alike that a spirit of contentment and loyalty should be encouraged to exist through all ranks. With this in mind, your company in addition to wages on a generous scale, inaugurated a gradual system providing not only extra wages for long and satisfactory service to the masters, mates and engineers of the fleet, but also a bonus system based on the profit of each voyage. The experience of this innovation was it attracted a superior type of man and it was proposed to extend this to all members of the crew."

During the First World War 1914-18 the Prince Line fleet consisted of 45 steamers of which 21 ships were lost through enemy or other maritime actions and 86 crew members lost their lives. The Portuguese Prince was normally engaged on the North America – South America service carrying principally coffee and cocoa beans from Brazil to New York but three months into the war she was converted and then carried 1200 two year old horses, along with 3000 tons of fresh water and fodder, hay and bran for the horses on a regular run from New York into Brest, France to aid the war effort.

3   Cullercoats connection

The first record I could find of James' interest in Cullercoats, a small fishing village, two miles north of North Shields, was in the Shields Daily News of 22 August 1883 which recorded how he presented a telescope to the Cullercoats Volunteer Life Brigade. The Brigade, the second in the country was formed on 8 December 1864 and by 1879 when the new watch house was built above the bay, its members, who were mainly local fishermen, totalled 110.

In 1886 a regatta was established at Cullercoats to encourage swimming amongst the fishermen, few of whom could swim. Another activity at the regatta was coble racing and Sir James who was an enthusiastic yachtsman and coble sailor was judge for this event. This may have been the start of his enthusiasm for the village. He also took part in a volunteer workforce to remove rocks from the vicinity of the north pier so it could be rebuilt.

In the Shields Daily Gazette of 7 June 1890, it records how Mr James Knott, a local philanthropist has purchased five acres of land on the north of Cullercoats Bay to erect thereon cottages for the fishermen.

Again in the Shields Daily Gazette, it reported "On Saturday 19 July 1890 the second of a series of three races between the yachting coble "Norma", owned by Mr S Watson of Newbiggin and the "Marguerite" owned by James Knott of Newcastle was sailed off Cullercoats. Mr Knott and Mr Watson agreed to race over a ten mile course on three consecutive Saturdays for a friendly wager of £10 a side. The competition was won by Mr Knott who very generously handed over the winning money to the fund for the restoration of Cullercoats south pier."

The following July, at the Cullercoats annual regatta on 14 July 1891 the first races of the season were held at Cullercoats. The first match for cobles, was thrice round a triangular course of nine knots between Messrs Ridley and Nelson of Sunderland in the "Regina", Mr Mastermann of South Shields in the "Proserpine", Mr Watson of Newbiggin in the "Norma" and Mr Knott of Cullercoats in the "Marguerite". Mr Knott won and he later presented a silver cup for the second match which was for yachts and boats.

By the beginning of the 20th century, Sir James' businesses had grown considerably and after moving from Alma Place in North Shields, at various times the family rented property in the Newcastle area including the Manor House at Jesmond from 1889 where Henry Basil Knott was born 5 February 1891.

On the Census return for 1891 along with the family members are listed nine servants including a French tutor for Sir James' sons, James and Henry.

Administrative County of Newcastle upon Tyne					The undermentioned Houses are situate within the Boundaries of the											
Civil Parish		Municipal Borough	Municipal Ward	Urban Sanitary District	Town or Village or Hamlet	Rural Sanitary District			Parliamentary Borough or Division	Ecclesiastical Parish or District						
of Jesmond		of NEWCASTLE-upon-TYNE	of Jesmond	Newcastle upon Tyne of	of	of			Newcastle upon Tyne	of Jesmond						

No. of Schedule	ROAD, STREET, &c., and No. or NAME of HOUSE	HOUSES			NAME and Surname of each Person	RELATION to Head of Family	CONDITION as to Marriage	AGE last Birthday		PROFESSION or OCCUPATION	Employer	Employed	Neither Employer nor Employed	WHERE BORN	(1) Deaf-and-Dumb (2) Blind (3) Lunatic, Imbecile or Idiot
83	Manor Ho Lodge				James K Jackson	Son	S							Rochester Northumberland	
84	Manor House	1			James Knott	Head	M	40		Shipowner, Ship broker and Manufacturers Law				Rochester Northumberland	
					Margaret A. do	Wife	M		36					Howdon do	
					James L. Knott	Son	S	8						Holmfirth Yorkshire	
					Henry B. do	Son	S	8 mo						North Shields Northumberland	
					Emile Malfait	Serv	S		25	Valet				Jesmond do	
					Anne Headmarsh do		S		41	Housekeeper				Ann France	
					James G Carson do		S	30		Butler				Netherwitton Northumberland	
					May Tomlinson do		Wd		44	Certificated Nurse				Alverton Yorkshire	
					Hannah Caulfield do		S			Cook				Hears Durham	
					Isabella Armstrong do		S		24	Nurse				Durham do	
					Margaret J Mayhew do		S		20	Housemaid				Sheffield Northumberland	
					Sarah J Stoker do		S		29	Upper Housemaid				Bingham do	
					Mary J M Barker do		S		24	Kitchen maid				Newcastle upon Tyne	
85	Tythe road Gardens	1			Sarah Stait	Head	Wd		53	Gas keeper				Evesham Worcestershire	
					Thomas B. do	Son	S	29		Post Office Clerk				Droitwich do	

Then while living at the Manor House, Jesmond, in 1891, 56 Beverley Terrace, Cullercoats, an attractive sea fronting terraced house was bought in the name of Mrs Margaret Annie Knott and in 1907 number 57 was purchased and the two houses were combined. The building was not known as Monks Haven until 1914, two years after they were sold. This was probably used as a weekend "cottage", which they owned for 21 years. This was the first home they actually owned as all other residences untill this time had been rented.

A fine copper relief in the entrance hall of a Cullercoats fishwife with her creel on her back is a reminder that James and his wife had a soft spot for Cullercoats fisherfolk. (this was stolen in 2010)

This is believed to be depicting Polly Donkin, born in Cullercoats in 1858, possibly the most famous of the Cullercoats fisherwomen and holder of the lifeboat service Victoria Cross for raising money for the lifeboat.

On the stairs at the head of the first landing is a small balcony with a metal Venetian form grill which has initials set in the centres of the panels. The first being *J* and the second *M* for James and Margaret.

When Lady Knott died one of the newspaper columnists said that he fondly remembers the last occasion on which he met her was at Close House. It was on the lawn, she was entertaining all the old fisherwomen of Cullercoats and was sitting amongst them as they sang "Tynemouth Abbey". In the days when most people ate a proper lunch the Cullercoats fishwives used the train to get to Newcastle before lunch to sell their fish. When the new electric train service between the coast and Newcastle started around 1903, the fishwives were compelled to use a special train. They then had a problem if their husband's boat was late in due to the weather because they missed their special train and the chance of selling their fish in Newcastle. James Knott made successful representation to the North Eastern Railway Company which allowed them to travel in the guards van of the electric train with their fresh fish. When the Channel Fleet visited the Tyne in September 1904 there were over 500 official invitations issued to officials and dignitaries for the many civic banquets and events to celebrate the event.

As an example of Sir James' affection for the people of Cullercoats he engaged the tug the "Lord Warden" to make two trips from the New Quay at North Shields on the afternoon of Tuesday 27 November 1904 to give the women of Cullercoats the opportunity of inspecting the vessels at anchor in the river. Another example of his generosity was that in 1900 he gave an accordion to Martin William Henderson who had been born in Cullercoats in 1880 and was almost blind from birth but had an early aptitude for music and was a piano player. With this instrument Martin was then able to pursue a successful music hall career billed as the 'Blind Musical Marvel' or 'The Concertina King' and he played the music halls throughout Europe and as far afield as Australia. He returned to Cullercoats in 1920 where he lived until his death in 1941.

In July 1899 James took delivery of a new yacht "Imogene", but in October of that year it was wrecked in the bay along with three other yachts during a storm. The Shields Daily News of 19 August 1903 recorded that as President of Rockcliffe Swimming Club James Knott attended the gala at Whitley Salt Baths. By 1906 he was President of the Cullercoats Amateur Swimming Club which at that time had 97 members and he was very involved with affairs concerning the village. At a public meeting that year he criticized the council for their neglect of the village, raising rents and failing to provide decent street lighting and maintaining the roads.

Monks Haven, Cullercoats and the coachhouse at the rear of the premises

During this period of depression and being aware of many men seeking employment, he had built a terrace of substantial houses on Marden Avenue, which leads inland from the harbour. This was not the act of a speculative property developer but typical of his care for his community and an attempt to provide some much needed employment.

A foundation laying ceremony took place on the 23 May 1899 for the new Primitive Methodist Church at Cullercoats which was required due to the increased congregation at the existing church. Amongst those invited were listed Mr and Mrs Knott of Jesmond.

It was recorded that "Mrs Knott had most cheerfully and willingly responded to the request to perform the ceremony" and after laying the foundation stone, Mrs Knott was presented with the silver trowel inscribed "Presented to Mrs James Knott on laying the foundation stone of the Primitive Methodist Church, Cullercoats, May 23 1899". A vote of thanks was given to Mr and Mrs Knott for the substantial help the trustees had received by their deepest interest in the work of the church. Mr James Knott in acknowledging the compliment said there was a saying that heaven helps those that help themselves and considering that that the fishermen who earned their living in such a precarious way, had started to build a chapel, it was privilege to be allowed to assist them.

On one of the shutters on the first fishermen's cottages in Front Street was a shrine with fresh flowers added daily and attached was list of fishermen lost at sea. The cottage was the home of Mrs Jacob Smith who also lost two sons, one in the war and one after the war when his trawler struck a mine and ever since the war she kept the shrine lovingly constantly cared for. James Knott was a friend of the family and never passed along the street without calling at the house, even after he moved away from Cullercoats, when in the area he would stop to talk about the old times when he and Lady Knott had their home in the village. Although one very poor and one very rich, they shared a common bond as they had both suffered the loss of their two sons as a result of the war.

Manor House, Jesmond

In 1897 the family moved from the Manor House, to 4 Syndham Terrace, St Andrews, Newcastle, a substantial three storied house which was demolished in the 1960s for the building of the motorway. In the 1901 Census they are recorded here and among the servants are listed a companion housekeeper and a ladies maid for Mrs Knott.

Whilst at Jesmond, Sir James was a member of Canon James Theodore Inskip's congregation at Clayton Memorial Church. Canon Inskip was later Bishop of Barking and although in a wheelchair following a recent accident, because of his friendship with Sir James, he travelled to Jersey to read the committal service at the graveside at Sir James' funeral service.

Sir James still retained his connections at the coast, in 1904 as President of the Inshore Fishermen's Protection Association he provided a supper for the members in Cullercoats Primitive Church school room. Then on 28 September 1906 he officially opened the new headquarters building of Whitley Bay Golf Course.

The connection continued even after his death, as on 6 June 1964, Lady Elizabeth Knott came to Cullercoats for the naming ceremony of the Sir James Knott lifeboat. She had been invited by the Sir James Knott Trust, who had funded the lifeboat, travelling from her home on Jersey to England and then on the overnight train from London. She presented the lifeboat to the RNLI on behalf of the Sir James Knott Trust, there followed various speeches then at the end of the formalities Her Grace The Duchess of Northumberland officially named the lifeboat.

In this picture the Duchess can be seen in the left of the officials' pavilion, wearing a white hat and Lady Knott can be seen standing on the right making her address.

The importance of this event to the local community can be seen by the crowds who came to witness this event, packing the beach and bank top. Inside the RNLI boathouse can still be seen the tablet mounted on the wall recording the lifeboat's actions when stationed at Cullercoats from 1963 to 1969.

The Sir James Knott being launched after the naming ceremony.

CONTINUATION OF SERVICES
RENDERED BY
THE CULLERCOATS LIFE-BOATS
OF THE
ROYAL NATIONAL LIFE-BOAT INSTITUTION.
THE SIR JAMES KNOTT LIFE-BOAT
sent to the station in November 1963. A gift
received from the SIR JAMES KNOTT TRUST
was used towards the cost of this life-boat.

1963 Nov 17 Motor Cruiser. Saved boat and   Rescued 2

1964 Feb 11 M/v Queensgate. Stood by vessel

1964 Feb 11 M/v Queensgate. Gave help

1964 May 20 Converted Ships Lifeboat
                              Saved boat and   3

1965 Aug 29 Motor dinghy and cabin cruiser
              FAITH . . . . . Escorted dinghy and
              gave help to FAITH.

1966 Aug 30 Polish Trawler SZKUNER . . Gave help

1966 Aug 30 Polish Trawler SZKUNER . . Gave help

1967 Sep 3 Motor Launch McGregor
             in tow of fishing boat.
                              Escorted boats

1968 Oct 12 Cabin Cruiser ROTHESAY
                              Saved boat and   3

             Fishing Boat TINA
                              Saved boat and   6

4

His other interests

Apart from shipping, Sir James had many other business interests. In 1899 he purchased Togston Colliery and formed the Acklington Coal Co Ltd, which was later taken over by Broomhill Colliery Ltd. He also had an interest in an anthracite mine called the South Wales Primrose Coal Co.

Always keep to improve himself, like his younger brother Matthew, who was a solicitor, in July 1885 he entered Gray's Inn to study law and became a barrister in 1889. To be admitted to Gray's Inn he would have had examinations in English Language, Latin and English History and then would have passed examinations in Roman and English Law. He practiced for about four years before returning to his first love, shipping. He was also a J.P. for Northumberland.

He was a keen gardener and enjoyed deep sea fishing and clinker built coble racing off the north-east coast and held tenancies for shooting purposes on various country estates in Durham. In later years he enjoyed sailing his private yacht around the Mediterranean.

As well as being a successful businessman, Sir James had always been a benefactor and a generous supporter of many charitable institutions. In 1888 he presented to the Mission to Deep Fishermen a vessel suitable for their work among fishing smacks working in the North Sea. The Newcastle Journal of 4 March 1902 recorded that "Mr James Knott of Newcastle and Cullercoats has made a generous gift to the Presbyterian Day School, Howard Street, North Shields. He was approached by a gentleman who requested a subscription from him towards the clearing of a debt upon the school. Mr Knott asked how much the debt was then at once made out a cheque for the whole amount, slightly over £200 and handed it to his visitor".

On 5 October 1904 he officially opened a grand bazaar in St.Augustin's Church, North Shields and when in 1905, the North Shields fishing vessel "Campville" was lost at sea he initiated a fund to support the wives and children of the crew. He also made donations to the Newcastle City Mission to provide clogs to women and children in the winters of 1904 and 1905. In 1899 he provided a James Knott Challenge Cup to be played for amongst Borough of Tynemouth Bowling Clubs which is still played for today.

Sir James wife Margaret was also very involved in charitable work and on 17 December 1902 she opened a sale of work to raise funds for the Tyne Mission to Seamen in the Victoria Hall, Fowler Street, South Shields. When Tynemouth Victoria Jubilee Infirmary in North Shields was struggling for vital funds, she donated a 50-guineas trophy, the Tynemouth Infirmary Senior Cup in 1905, the receipts from the competition games to be given to the infirmary.

Sir James Knott has been described as a strong, genial, vigorous, enthusiastic and courageous man, always keen to take advantage of changing technical advances in shipping and business generally. He was noted to have a retentive memory and to be very observant, studious and a reader of a wide range of books particularly about the wars of Europe and the life of Napoleon. His was said by his contemporaries to be the most genial of friends. He had been a director of the Newcastle Protection and Indemnity Association from the inception of the club in 1886. (This is an insurance scheme operated by shipping companies for their own protection.) He was a Knight of Grace of the Order of St.John of Jerusalem in England and Vice President of the Northern Counties Orphanage. He was President and a patron of the Prudhoe Gleeman Choir when the choir began in Wylam in 1903.

He was a regular attender at church and an ardent Conservative. He was also an ardent Unionist and keen tariff reformer, and was one of the founders of the Northern Tariff Reform Federation. This was a protectionist British pressure group formed in 1903 to protest against what they considered to be unfair foreign imports and to advocate Imperial Preference to protect British industry from foreign competition. The League wanted to see the British Empire transformed into a single trading bloc, to compete with Germany and the United States and proposed imposing duties on imports and the channelling of the money raised from these duties into social reforms. In June 1901 when the Select Committee of the House of Common were inquiring into the effect "foreign subsidies had upon the British shipping trade" they called upon James Knott to give evidence as the representative of the North of England Steamship Owners Association.

He seems now to have been politically active for on 27 of October 1903 at the Tynemouth Conservative Club Debating Society, James held an open discussion on "Shipping trades that have been lost to this district by the unfair methods of foreign Governments" and in January 1905 he gave an illustrated lecture entitled "Our Empire" in Chirton School room, North Shields and in St.George's Hall, Cullercoats.

In the Shields Daily News of 22 February 1905 it stated that it had been suggested his shipping line, as with other shipping lines, after taking their ships to foreign ports would pay off their crews there and engage cheaper foreign crews. James said he was prepared to give £100 (equivalent to £13,000 today) to any charity if it was proved the Prince Line was not better manned and the men not better fed, housed and paid than two local well known large shipping lines managed by Liberals. In January 1906 there was a series of letters published by James Knott and Walter Runciman (another prominent local shipowner) in a public dispute over their crews' conditions.

On the 10 June 1905 James became an Honorary Lieutenant in the Royal Navy Volunteer Reserve, a position he held until 1927. At the outbreak on the 1914-18 War he was not called up, as his position in the shipping industry was considered so important to the war effort.

James must have been impressed with Joseph Chamberlain's campaign for tariff reforms which was launched by Chamberlain in the autumn of 1903 and so stood in January 1906 for the Tyneside Division which covered a large area from Lemington and Benwell in the west, Gosforth, Seaton Burn, Walker, Wallsend and Willington Quay in the east. Before 1912 Members of Parliament were not paid and so needed a private income and fortunately James possessed a motor car for such a widespread constituency and could speak at two or three meetings a day. He travelled through this area in his car, brightly decked in red and conspicuously bearing his flag of the Prince Line. He was unsuccessful in this election, gaining 6,885 votes, but the Liberal candidate polled 11,496. He was not disheartened by his defeat and continued to be an active speaker at many meetings particularly those of the Primrose League. This was an organisation for spreading Conservative principles in Great Britain founded in 1883 whose membership was said to be well over a million by the early 1890s and at that time enjoyed more support than the British trade union movement. Its aims were to support God, Queen, and Country and the Conservative cause; provide an effective voice to represent the interests of their members for the common good; to encourage and help its members to improve their professional competence as leaders and to fight for free enterprise.

On 15 February 1909, as President of the All Saints Conservative Club in Newcastle, he delivered an interesting and forcible address on tariff reforms and the state of trade in continental countries which placed constraints on industrial conditions in this country. When challenged about the accuracy of his statement he advised he had travelled extensively visiting America, Germany, Belgium, France, Italy and Holland to check for himself working conditions abroad.

He stood again in January 1910 as Conservative MP for Sunderland, this being a relevant constituency for him as he had Prince Line ships built on the Wear, which no doubt helped gain him votes. He again stood on the tariff reform platform and was duly elected. He wrote a letter to the Sunderland Daily Echo on 16 November 1910 saying "with the greatest reluctance I will be unable to be a Parliamentary candidate for Sunderland at the coming election. My health has been unsatisfactory since the last election, when Sunderland did me the great honour of sending me to Parliament as one of its representatives but my medical advisors have now forbidden me to undertake the arduous task of going through another contest following on closely as it does upon the last and particularly in mid-winter. I cannot tell you how deeply and sincerely and with what reluctance I am laying down the position with which the people of Sunderland honoured me, the duties of which I have tried faithfully to fulfil and the position which I have been so proud to occupy – yours faithfully, James Knott". He retired in December 1910, to focus on his businesses.

An article in the Newcastle Journal of Thursday 25 August 1910 reported that "speaking at the foundation laying of the additions to St.Ebba Church Ebchester, yesterday, Mr James Knott, MP who referred to his presence there as being a mark of friendship to the vicar, who was formerly a schoolboy acquaintance of his, delivered a stirring address on British manhood and the powerful influence that education and discipline had exercised in moulding that national character of sturdiness for which Britishers were famed and admired throughout the world. Alluding to the ancient history of the church, which represented forty generations of folk, he hoped and believed that the old spirit and tradition of their ancestors inbued the company there assembled in carrying on the cause of religion and education."

The vicar, the charismatic Rev. John George Gibson as a boy lived at 33 Bird Street, North Shields a few streets from James in Linskill Street and they both attended the school attached to the Scotch Church nearby in Howard Street.

In 1914 when the training ship Wellesley, moored at North Shields, caught fire he gave £1,000 towards its restoration.

It was reported in the Liverpool Journal of Commerce on 4 November 1916 that Mr James Knott has retired from the position of Vice-President of the North of England Steamship Owners Association. He presented to the Newcastle Exchange an oil painting of his first vessel, the brig Pearl.

By 1906 they moved from Jesmond to **Close House, Wylam**. Close House mansion was built in 1779, and the estate covered an area of 606 acres of land and 11 acres of water. Close House estate was originally owned by the Radcliffe family, and it passed to the Read family at some time between 1412-24. It was sold by the Reads to Robert Bewicke in 1620 and became the seat of the Bewicke family, who lived there for the next 333 years. It was during the temporary absence of the Bewickes that Close House was leased from the Bewicke family, initially for a period of five years, the lease was later extended up to the period when Sir James moved to Jersey in 1925.

On this 1911 Census of Close House are listed James and Margaret, their two younger sons James and Henry, a visitor Norton Butler Napier Good (naval architect) and eleven servants.

CENSUS OF ENGLAND AND WALES, 1911.

Name and Surname	Relationship to Head of Family	Age	Particulars as to Marriage					Profession or Occupation				Birthplace
James Knott	Head	56	Married	34	3	3		Shipowner	567		Employer	Howdon-on-Tyne
Margaret Annie Knott	Wife	56	do	34	3	3						Holmfirth, Yorkshire
James Leadbitter Knott	Son	28	Single					Shipowner	567		Employer	North Shields, Northumberland
Henry Basil Knott	Son	20	Single					Shipowner Clerk	050	547	Worker	Jesmond, Newcastle, Northumberland
Norton Butler Napier Good	Visitor	24	Single					Naval Architect	080		Worker	St Pauls, Bromley, London
William Graham	Servant	42	Single					Butler	Domestic		Worker	Brampton, Cumberland
Mary Graham	Servant	45	Married	9				Cook	Domestic		Worker	Peling, Edinburgh
Arthur Sanderson	Servant	21	Single					Footman	Domestic		Worker	Southshore, Yorkshire
Evelyn Twiddell	Servant	18	Single					Kitchen Maid	Domestic		Worker	Burnopfield, Durham
Margaret Jane Bowman	Servant	18	Single					House Maid			Worker	Hexhamshire, Hexham
Mabel Morrow	Servant	18	Single					Scullery Maid			Worker	Starbottle, Yorkshire
Elizabeth Sharp	Servant	17	Single					Lady Housekeeper			Worker	York, Yorkshire
Caroline Jane Cowing	Servant	34	Single					Housemaid			Worker	Gateshead-on-Tyne
Isabella Sanderson	Servant	29	Single					Chauffeur	077		Worker	Keswick, Cumberland
Sidney Robinson Rothwaite	Servant	28	Single					Lady's Maid	010		Worker	Hull, Shields
Mary Annie Heslop	Servant	32	Single					Lady's Maid	010		Worker	

James had certainly come a long way from when a boy, in his humble Tyneside flat in North Shields.

Sir James Knott.

Close House,
Wylam.

CLOSE HOUSE, WYLAM.

With best wishes for
Christmas and the
New Year.

Xmas, 1918.

His sons

5

James Leadbitter Knott born on 2 December 1882 at 1 Frank Place, North Shields was educated at Eton from 1896 to 1900 and was described as widely travelled, some of which as part of his training in the Prince Line business to find how shipping of goods was conducted particularly in the United States and South America. He went to the USA several times, on three occasions staying for three months and it was said he knew New York, Boston and Philadelphia as well as he knew Newcastle. For eight months he lived in British and Portuguese South Africa and he travelled extensively in Holland, Belgium, Germany, Austro-Hungary, France, Bulgaria, Turkey, Italy, Egypt and North Africa. In 1906, at the age of 24, his father made him a partner in the management company renaming it James Knott and Son and in 1914 was made deputy managing director. He was also a director of the Newcastle Daily Journal, was an active participant in the social and political life of Newcastle and a political activist supporting fair trade and fiscal reform like his father. He was one of the chief hopes of the Unionist Party in the North. He was an enthusiastic sportsman excelling in rowing and shooting and supporter of charitable organisations and a member of the Natural History Society of Northumbria. When the government declared was against Germany in 1914 there was national wave of nationalism and a general rush to enlist. Both James and Basil enlisted on 8 August, then on 10 September 1914 James became a second Lieutenant in the 4th Battalion of the Northumberland Fusiliers then on 21 November was made a captain in the 9th Battalion Northumberland Fusiliers. Then on 22 December 1915 he was promoted to major and second in command in the 10th Battalion of the Prince of Wales Own West Yorkshire Regiment. As second in command of his battalion he would be aware of how challenging the proposed Somme offensive would be. He was awarded the Distinguished Service Order (DSO) for military service in the birthday honours on 3 June 1916.

James Leadbitter Knott

Henry Basil Knott

Henry Basil Knott, or "Pomp" as he was known to his family, was born in the family home, Manor House, Jesmond on 5 January 1891 and baptised 18 April 1891 at St.George's Church, Jesmond. After education for six years at Eton he left aged 19 to train in his father's business becoming responsible for the coal trade department, was a director of a coal company, a businessman at Newcastle Commercial Exchange, was popular in private and business life and was a clever caricaturist and regular contributor to the local press. In 1914 his father made him a partner in the ship management company James Knott and Son renaming it James Knott, Sons and Company Ltd. After enlisting in August 1914, giving his military experience as four years as a private in Eton College Volunteers, on 10 September he became a second lieutenant in the 4th Battalion Northumberland Fusiliers. In November he was made lieutenant in the 9th Battalion Northumberland Fusiliers and on 1 June 1915 just before going to France was promoted to Captain. His battalion crossed the channel on 15 July and by 5 September were at the front.

Henry was fatally wounded the next day and was taken to the casualty station at Poperinghe at 10pm and died four hours later, less than two months after landing in Flanders. He was buried in the military cemetery in Poperinghe.

After Henry died on 7 September 1915, James was given an appointment in the control of shipping which would have given him a safe position for the duration of the war. He was pressed to accept this position but felt unable to and returned to his unit. On the 1 July 1916, a day when no doubt his parents would be celebrating the news that he had been appointed a Justice of the Peace for the city of Newcastle, he wrote a moving letter to his father on the first day of the Battle of the Somme. He said he had been thinking of his brother and that he might be joining him and for Sir James not to think badly of him for refusing safe employment and to forgive him if it gives him grief at the death of two of his sons. He had a strong Christian faith as shown in this very moving letter dated the 1 July 1916, it reads:

"My dearest Father and Mother If you are reading this letter it means that this war has demanded the extreme sacrifice from me, and my object in writing is to bring you, as far as I can, some measure of consolation and courage and patience to bear your sorrow.

It is not in any sense a message from the grave because I have very complete faith in the Life Eternal. I know that I will be with you when you are reading this, and I want you to realise, and always remember that, although Providence has decided that I may not return to you in the flesh, that I shall be always with you in spirit sharing your joys and sorrows.

I feel compelled by my knowledge of you both to write this, because my own great anxiety at the present time is the thought of your grief and the possibility of your collapse if I follow 'Pomp'. Momentous events are looming up and I have a premonition that I may not return to you. I have been dreaming of Basil recently, and I have an indistinct recollection of a letter in Basil's handwriting dated June 1916, which I feel is his warning and message. If I am correct then you will both know Basil and I are happy.

I hope and desire above all things that you will not unduly grieve. You must not think harshly of me for refusing to accept safe employment, even if my action results in my death and your sorrow. We have all to show courage – those out here in facing the music and taking what comes in a stoic manner – those at home in facing the loneliness that must follow he casualties of severe fighting.

I do want you to know and to realise how deeply and whole heartedly I have appreciated and loved you both for your unselfish devotion and all-forgiving love. My life has been one uninterrupted period of all that a man could wish for or desire. If I die now I am content to do so. Life is sweet, and holds out all that a young man could desire – power, wealth and above all, great love, but I want you to know that I faced the future fearlessly, and that I was cheerful and satisfied.

My medals are yours but I should like them destroyed when you both join me – whenever that may be. Always remember that I am relying on you both to be good brave parents and that I can only be really happy in a new life if I know and can see that you are happy too. My clothes, furniture and motor car must all be immediately disposed of, everything which reminds you of my death must be removed – this is my urgent desire and wish. God grant that you will be given good health, strength and happiness for many years. Your devoted son   JIM".

James was killed later that same day, aged just 32 along with over 700 men of his Battalion. In his will published in September 1915 he left £104,350.

The two brothers are remembered: on the war memorial in front of St.George's Church, Cullercoats, just a few hundred yards from their earlier home at Monks Haven.

On the war memorial on the village green in Wylam village.

In York Minster in the Memorial Chapel to the West Yorkshire Regiment, Sir James presented wrought iron screens with a dedicatory brass plaque to his sons, Major and Captain Knott.

Cullercoats memorial

Wylam village war memorial

So the Knott family lost two sons, both serving officers in France during the First World War.

At the end of the war Sir James and Lady Knott waged a lengthy campaign to have the bodies of their sons returned to England but the Government decided that if allowed, only wealthy families would benefit so this was not allowed. But despite being killed almost a year apart, and being buried around 70 miles from each other, the brothers were eventually reunited and buried side by side in Reservoir Cemetery at Ypres which is quite unusual, as tradition dictated that British servicemen were traditionally buried where they died. Sir James must have exerted considerable pressure to enable his two younger sons to be buried like this.

Their gravestones each bear the same inscription *'Devoted In Life In Death Not Divided'* which was chosen by the Knott family. After their deaths, Sir James Knott, donated the bell tower at St George's Memorial Church in Ypres, Belgium. The images below show the memorial stones at St.George's Memorial Church, where the bell was to be rung in memory of the Knott brothers.

Sir James Knott was devastated by the death of his sons James and Henry, both of whom had been educated at Eton College then became directors in the family shipping company and oldest son Garbutt also being reported missing in action. So it was believed that all of his sons had been killed in this War. Having built up this substantial shipping empire he obviously expected to hand over control to his sons in the future and it may be because of their deaths and also the death of his brother Stanley, who had also served in France, that these tragic events were the main reason he decided to sell the Prince Line. He sold his shipping empire to Furness, Withy & Co. West Hartlepool Ship-owners at the end of 1916 for £3million (£270 million today), then to establish and endow the Knott Memorial Trust, initially to help the widows of men killed in battle. Furness Withy was an excellent choice to become the new custodian of the Prince Line and they operated the fleet as a separate part of their larger fleet. The Price Line livery, house flag and naming nomenclature were retained only adding a thin red line to the funnels.

It has been written **Thomas Garbutt Knott**, or Garbutt as he was known, born 14 July 1879 at 6 Frank Place, North Shields, the oldest son, was the black sheep of the family. I think this is unfair just because Thomas had not had a good relationship with his father after they reputedly quarrelled when he refused to join the family business. At the age of 12 he had been boarded and tutored by the Rev. James Lemmon, a Scottish Presbyterian minister at West Thirston near Felton, Northumberland and it may have been that his father wanted him to have the same education as he had received at the Scotch Presbyterian Church in North Shields. However, his two younger brothers, were educated at Eton, England's leading public school and Sir James could have afforded for all three sons to have gone there and then after a first class education given them all a secure future as directors in their father's business empire. Thomas may not have passed Eton's entrance examination or been suited to an administrative career but at the age of 16 he was apprenticed to Robert Fernie, a Liverpool ship-owner and director of a shipping line which specialised in transporting immigrants to America which may have given him knowledge of foreign ports in America and wanderlust. He did seem to be an adventurous wanderer and departed to South Africa in 1899 aged 20, when his brothers were aged 17 and 8, working his passage as a deck hand on one of his father's ships after his father refused him free passage. He may have gone there to meet his Uncle Stanley, his father's younger brother who had gone there initially in about 1890 returning in 1893 before returning and fighting in the Boer War 1899-1902. Whilst back home Thomas may have spoken to his uncle or tales of his exploits may have encouraged him to travel there and he also fought in the Boer War enlisting in the South African Light Horse from 1899 to 1902.

On the road from North Shields to Cullercoats stands Tynemouth Congregational Church and inside is a large brass tablet recording the names of over 200 local men who went to fight in the South African campaign. Below the main tablet is attached a smaller tablet with another seven names who had been omitted from the main tablet. Among these are Thomas G Knott and his Uncle Stanley.

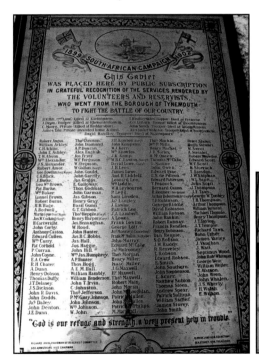

By 1902 he is in America, recorded as a labourer on 11 October 1907, marrying at the Empire Hall, Ashtabula, Sara Elizabeth Fowler a divorcee, who had been married three times before, in Ashtabula, Ohio. It was a poor marriage and in 1912 his wife petitioned for divorce citing his violent behaviour and he cross petitioned to divorce her for unreasonable behaviour. The Judge declared there was insufficient evidence to support both claims and refused to grant either party a divorce. Thomas decided to travel again and by 1913 was in Sydney, Australia but his wife had refused to go with him.

With the death of his two younger sons, who had been expected to inherit the business, Sir James may have believed that his considerable fortune would now pass to Thomas, whose estranged wife in America would have a claim on part of the fortune. She was certainly aware that Thomas came from a wealthy family as during her unsuccessful attempt to divorce him in 1912 she told the court that he was "continually in receipt of large sums of money from his parents who live in England". This may be why rumours of Thomas's death were allowed to circulate but these payments do prove that although he had apparently fallen out with his father he had not been disowned. At a memorial service for Major James Knott in July 1916 in Newcastle Cathedral, sympathy was extended to "Mr and Mrs Knott who have been bereft of their entire family of three gallant soldiers". As well as having lost the two younger sons on the Western Front it was widely reported that their eldest son Thomas was also a victim being described as being killed, wounded, missing or taken prisoner by the Germans.

When war broke out in 1914 Thomas was living in Clinton a small town on South Island, New Zealand, and enlisted on 14 August in the Otago Mounted Rifles as a trooper stating he was not married and giving his father's name as next of kin. He was promoted to corporal eight weeks later then sailed from New Zealand on the troopship "Hawkes Bay" and disembarked in the Egyptian port of Alexandria on 3 December 1914. In Egypt during training he was reprimanded for having a light in his tent after hours and at his own request reverted to the rank of trooper in March 1915. By August he was taking part in the second offensive at Gallipoli and on 23 August he was wounded and transferred to a hospital on the Aegean island of Lemnos. On 1 October he was fit enough to rejoin his unit, then in July 1916 he transferred to the Anzac Camel Corp, then to the Auckland Rifles and served in the Egyptian Theatre of Operations with the Expeditionary Force from 1914-1918.

Thomas's movements and de-mob record.

He had been invalided to a hospital in Egypt with memory loss, then after news of his brothers' deaths reached him in 1916, meaning his family must have been aware of his location despite rumours of his death circulating back home, he was given two months compassionate leave from October 1917 to January 1918 to return to England as his mother's health had been affected by her sons' deaths. For a private soldier to be given such leave was unheard of and it may be that again his father pulled strings to facilitate it. At the end of the war he requested that he be demobbed in London rather than returning to New Zealand to be discharged at Clinton with his regiment. His commanding officer granted his request on 27 May 1919 and he took up residence in his father's house, Wylam Lodge in Torquay.

Thomas's wife believing he was dead and that it was therefore legal to do so, remarried in 1920. In 1924 Thomas reappeared having apparently recovered from his memory loss and divorced her on grounds of adultery to make sure she had no claim on him.

6   His developing philanthropic character

After the loss of his two sons, Sir James channelled his energy into many charitable acts. In 1918, Sir James bought much property in Heddon village from the trustees of the Clayton family, after the tenants' rents were increased, presumably with funds from the sale of his shipping empire. In 1924 he sold 32 lots of property in Heddon, about half of the village, including East Town Farm, Clayton Terrace, Blue Row, Garden House, the Blacksmiths shop and the Three Tuns Inn, selling some properties to the tenants at a low price. When this sale was announced the Society of Antiquaries of Newcastle asked him to donate the exposed stretch of the Roman Wall, which he did, and they made him an honorary member of the society.

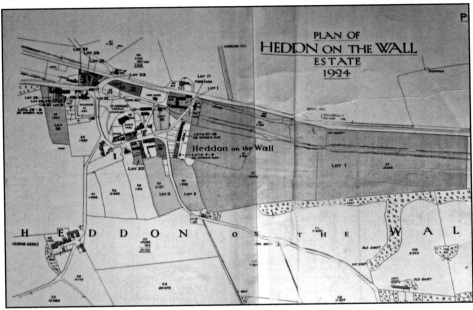

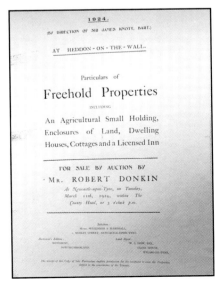

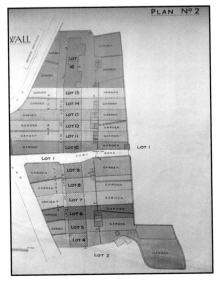

Did Sir James have a grand plan for Heddon? It seems strange that he should buy so much of the village. It has been suggested that Sir James wanted St Andrew's Church rededicated to St.James and St.Basil named after his sons and he could not get his way on this matter, so he sold his properties in the village. So then in 1926 money was donated instead for the building of the St.James and St.Basil church in Fenham , including the vicarage, church hall and a sunken garden.

In 1925 the Memorial Park at Heddon was laid out at the expense of Sir James Knott and was officially opened on 11 November 1925 and presented to the Heddon-on-the-Wall Parish Council by Sir James and Lady Knott in memory of their two sons: Major James Leadbitter Knott D.S.O. 10th West Yorkshire Regiment and Captain Henry Basil Knott 9th Northumberland Fusiliers, who were killed in action in the Great War. Within the garden is the war memorial.

The Church of St.Andrew is situated in the centre of the village on a hill top behind the Memorial Garden. The church was consecrated in 630AD and still retains many Saxon and later Norman elements. There is an early Norman chancel and rib-vaulted east bay with heavy reconstruction during the Early English period (1189-1280 approx). There is a Preaching Cross displayed below the Norman window and there are two decorative capitals on the North arcade. Such chunky capitals would be unusual in an Early English arcade and the decorations do not look at all late Norman. The church believes that they were recovered from a disused Roman building. There are elaborate stained glass windows given by Sir James Knott in memory of his two sons and a plaque to their memory.

During the 1914-18 war, Holeyn Hall in Wylam was used as a Military Hospital for wounded soldiers and Sir James arranged for a supply of cigarettes, tobacco and newspapers to be supplied for the patients. A nearby cottage later named Merci Beaucoup cottage was at that time unoccupied and Sir James Knott secured the tenancy of it, furnished it and provided food and it was opened as a guest house for wives and mothers of wounded soldiers invalided in Holeyn Hall where they could have a short stay, to visit their dear ones.

Lady Margaret Annie Knott was renowned for her modesty and good works and was a lifelong supporter of the welfare of women and children in reduced circumstances. It was said that only those who benefited by her widespread generosity knew of her kindness. She regularly entertained war widows and the dependants of ex-serviceman at Wylam and Heddon and had a lifelong interest in the Tynemouth Victoria Jubilee Infirmary, North Shields and the Fleming Memorial Children's Hospital, Newcastle. She also was a generous supporter of the Northern Counties Society for granting annuities to governesses and ladies in reduced circumstances and with Sir James, endowed and maintained two cots in memory of their sons at the Northern Counties Orphanage.

Merci Beaucoup cottage

After selling his shipping business he channelled his energy into his many interests including renovating the house and gardens at Close House, spending his summers at the appropriately named Wylam Lodge in Torquay.

In the Birthday Honours List of 1917 in recognition of his life's work he was made a Baronet and became Sir James Knott Bt. His Coat of Arms bore the words 'Facta non Verba' which appropriately translates to 'Deeds not words'. After receiving a letter of congratulations from the Lord Mayor and members of Newcastle City Council, he wrote them a letter saying, "My wife and I were greatly touched by the message from the Council. If kindness would soften blows then indeed we should hardly feel the effect of them. It is all so sad, without our sons to share it, it seems futile".

In May 1919 he sent a cheque of £1,500 to pay for two places, one boy and one girl in memory of his late sons at the Northern Counties Orphanage, Moor Edge, Newcastle where he was Vice-President. In 1928 he gave £6,000 for the building of a new swimming baths at the orphanage. Also in 1919 at a meeting of the Comrades of the Great War charity in Blyth, of which he was Honorary President, Sir James offered to erect cottages for the widows and dependants of members of the Northumbrian Fusilier Regiment in which his sons had also served and died. This offer was not taken up.

Another generous offer which didn't come to fruition was when in 1920 Newcastle Council proposed the building of a war memorial in Eldon Square, Sir James suggested instead a larger memorial incorporating a 100 foot high column on the Town Moor and offered £20,000 towards its construction. However, this was rejected by the Council stating a smaller memorial in Eldon Square built by public subscription was more appropriate.

In 1920 he set up a Settlement Trust, described in an sixteen page Indenture dated 18 November, to provide for Thomas Garbutt and any issue that he may have and also if he should die without heirs or dependants, money from the trust should be given to charitable causes.

It arranged for funds to be made available by trustees of his investments "for the building of two churches for the Church of England, one at Newsham to be called St.James Church and the other at Shiremoor to be called St.Basil's Church both in the County of Northumberland together with a vicarage and church hall for each such church in such places in the said County as the Trustees shall at their absolute discretion decide and so that the said church at Newsham, Blyth, shall have an endowment of £600 per annum and the said church to be built at Shiremoor shall have an endowment of £500 per annum such endowments to be paid out of income of the Trust Fund".

The indenture also stipulated that in the church there should be a memorial in white marble with black lettering stating that the church had been built in the memory of Major James Leadbitter Knott who gave his life for his country in the Great War and a similar memorial in the church to be built at Shiremoor with an inscription stating that it had been built in memory of Captain Henry Basil Knott who gave his life for his country in the Great War. The indenture went on to stipulate if either of these churches were not possible then another, or others, should be built in the Diocese of Northumberland where the trustees should select.

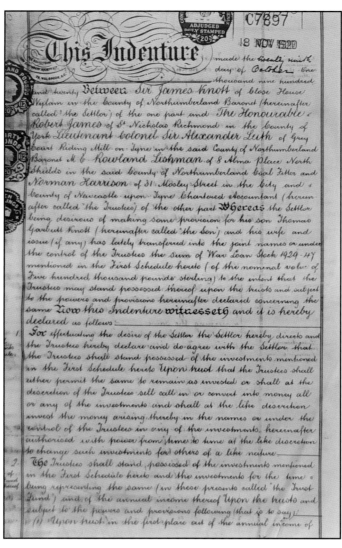

This Indenture

made the twenty ninth day of October One thousand nine hundred and twenty **Between** Sir James Knott of Close House Wylam in the County of Northumberland Baronet (hereinafter called "the Settlor") of the one part and The Honourable Robert James of St Nicholas Richmond in the County of York Lieutenant Colonel Sir Alexander Leith of Grey Court Riding Mill on Tyne in the said County of Northumberland Baronet M C Rowland Lishman of 8 Alma Place North Shields in the said County of Northumberland Coal Fitter and Norman Harrison of 31 Mosley Street in the City and County of Newcastle upon Tyne Chartered Accountant (hereinafter called "the Trustees") of the other part **Whereas** the Settlor being desirous of making some provision for his son Thomas Garbutt Knott (hereinafter called "the Son") and his wife and issue (if any) has lately transferred into the joint names or under the control of the Trustees the sum of War Loan Stock 1929-47 mentioned in the First Schedule hereto (of the nominal value of Five hundred thousand pounds sterling) to the intent that the Trustees may stand possessed thereof upon the trusts and subject to the powers and provisions hereinafter declared concerning the same **Now this Indenture witnesseth** and it is hereby declared as follows:—

1. For effectuating the desire of the Settlor the Settlor hereby directs and the Trustees hereby declare and do agree with the Settlor that the Trustees shall stand possessed of the investments mentioned in the First Schedule hereto Upon trust that the Trustees shall either permit the same to remain as invested or shall at the discretion of the Trustees sell call in or convert into money all or any of the investments and shall at the like discretion invest the money arising thereby in the names or under the control of the Trustees in any of the investments hereinafter authorised with power from time to time at the like discretion to change such investments for others of a like nature

2. The Trustees shall stand possessed of the investments mentioned in the First Schedule hereto and the investments for the time being representing the same (in these presents called "the First Fund") and of the annual income thereof Upon the trusts and subject to the powers and provisions following (that is to say)

(1) Upon trust in the first place out of the annual income of

---

reference only and shall not affect the construction thereof

In witness whereof the persons parties hereto have hereunto set their hands and seals the day and year first hereinbefore written

The First Schedule above referred to.

Particulars of Investments previously transferred into the joint names or under the control of the Trustees

£500,000 War Loan £5 per cent Stock 1929-47.

The Second Schedule above referred to.

Particulars of the nature or class of charitable purposes and religious purposes (being also charitable purposes recognised or permitted by law to be selected by the Trustees in giving effect to the trusts hereof if the ultimate trust hereinbefore contained in default of issue of the Son takes effect

(1) The building erection or reconstruction of buildings or other

47

The church authorities did not approve these locations so on 28 July 1928 the foundation stone was laid for the building of St James and St Basil's Church, church hall and vicarage in Fenham, Newcastle. It was consecrated on 6 June 1931 with the vicarage and parish hall completed in1932.

The whole complex, furnishing and fittings was a gift from Sir James to the parish which was seeking to build a new church. Besides this undoubtedly generous gesture, the gift was also to be a memorial to his two sons lost in the Great War, There was some unease at the time at the scale and nature of his gift, which was a combination of genuine philanthropy, a war memorial and a family shrine, since Sir James also lost his wife during the course of building. It is one of the great churches of the arts and crafts movement and recognised as a masterpiece, is grade II listed and said to be built with stone from John Dobson's 1830 Newcastle prison, in Carliol Square which was being demolished at that time.

The architect was Eric Edward Loftus of London who was an assistant surveyor to the fabric of Westminster Abbey. An unusual feature of its construction is a double sized main roof to confirm it was built in memory of two people. The tenor bell inside the church bears the inscription 'We ring in memory of James and Basil Knott, God knows'. A superb stained-glass window bears the images of his sons and at the top are depictions of Eton School and Close House and another stained glass window on the west wall is dedicated to Margaret Annie Knott.

When Sir James visited the north to see the progress of the building of the church he saw opposite to the church entrance a piece of vacant ground. He then purchased this land and had it laid out as a sheltered sunken garden of rest for the old, weary or infirm out of the wind. The organ, considered to be one of the finest in Newcastle was installed in 1931 as a memorial gift by Sir James and he also donated a collection of silver crosses, plates and vases for use in the church. These were made by John Paul Cooper, an associate of Sir James who was an architect and a leading craftsman in the arts and crafts movement who specialised in metalwork and jewellery. This collection is believed to be the largest collection of his silverware in existence. The two emblems of the church can be seen carved in wood and in the windows, the cockle shell, the emblem of St.James the Apostle and the dove, the emblem of St.Basil, Bishop of Caesarea. The finest craftsmen were brought to Fenham for its construction, many being unemployed ex-servicemen and former ship's carpenters.

In the Parish Hall are displayed portraits of Sir James, Lady Margaret, James and Henry, along with copies of James and Henry's medals.

James   Henry

Sir James   Lady Margaret

In 1924 Sir James Knott purchased Samares Manor on the island of Jersey which dates back to at least the 12th century and extensively refurbished the house and gardens.

He became the forty third Seigneur of Samares, the first believed to have been granted by Wiliam II in 1025. Seigneur is French for Lord. With the loss of his sons and the selling of his business empire he had no need to remain in Newcastle and in 1925 he retired there. The dining room was panelled in French walnut decorated with elaborate limewood carving and contained family portraits and landscape paintings. He reputedly spent around £50,000 on the gardens alone, between 1925 and his death in 1934, employing an expert landscape architect and forty gardeners to turn fifteen acres of the grounds into what is now one of the show places of the island. Two large ponds were created and plants were brought in from all over the world. From the interest he had taken in rock gardens in Japan, he had a rock garden built with limestone quarried in Cumberland, then transported to Jersey in two ship loads. He was immensely proud of his garden and there is a local story that he offered a pound to anyone who could find a weed in his gardens and he never had to pay it.

He also took a keen interest in the local breed of Jersey cattle and some of his herd was successfully exhibited at the Royal Jersey Show. He also spent his leisure time in yachting, his first acquisition being the 20 ton auxiliary ketch "Sunbeam".

Samares gardens

Later in 1924 he had a lovely 180 foot long, 30.1 feet broad and 730 tons gross, motor yacht aptly named "Princess" built by Furness Shipbuilding Co Ltd on the Tees. Among other things she had the facility to carry his Rolls Royce in her hold. She was first registered in Jersey on 23 April 1924. The walls and ceilings of the smoke room were a small scale reproduction of the famous Bromley room in the South Kensington Museum. In the dining room the furniture was finely carved mahogany based on the latter half of the eighteenth century and the drawing room was of very delicate detail of the Adam period. A letter he wrote to a friend, Charles Lawson on 25 December 1925 was on letterhead titled Yacht "Princess" Monaco Harbour. The yacht was transferred to Samares Investments with Sir James as its managing director but in 1926 he re-registered the yacht from the company to his name so it could fly the Blue Ensign. The Blue Ensign flag flown at the stern of a ship can only be flown on vessels in public service or commanded by an officer in the Royal Navy Reserve.

After Sir James' death the "Princess" was requisitioned for naval service in the war as an anti- submarine yacht in 1939 and the next year on 11 January 1940 she was in collision in the Bristol Channel with s.s. Blairmore (4141grt) and sank.

MY Princess   and   Sir James binoculars

She had made her will in 1928 appointing Rowland Lishman as one of her trustees leaving him an annuity of £50 if he would carry out her wishes and continue as a trustee as long as necessary. In her will she left £140,000 and requested her pearls and jewellery be sold and the proceeds given to the Northern Counties Society, founded in 1868 by Sir John Fife to give annuities to governesses and other ladies in reduced circumstances. Her godchildren, Malcolm (the son of her niece Francis Katherine Hunter), Nancy Howle, Nancy Murray and Elizabeth Dibb along with her cousin Herbert Gibson, her friends Mary Ann Hind and Elizabeth Evers were also all left legacies. After other bequests to the Northern Women's Hospital, the Hospital for Sick Children, the Fleming Memorial Hospital, the Sanderson Home for Crippled Children, all in Newcastle and the Officers' Families Fund in London, the remainder was gifted to her son Thomas Garbutt Knott. Her servants too were not forgotten and also received legacies, so even after her death she continued to support those charities she helped during her lifetime.

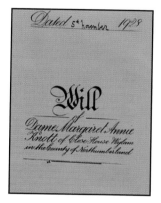

After the death of Lady Margaret, Sir James arranged for the continuation of entertainments, originally established by her, for the relatives of ex-soldiers in the parishes of Wylam-on-Tyne and Heddon-on-the –Wall, one in each per year. The whole cost of the events including transport and engagement of entertainers to be paid for by Samares Investments. There should also be presents, similar to those given by Lady Knott, for giving to each relation at Christmas. In 1930, he arranged for the purchase of flowers for the placing on the graves of himself and Lady Knott weekly and on those of his sons in Ypres Reservoir Cemetery.

After Lady Margaret's death, Sir James made a new will leaving some personal effects to Thomas and made several grants to her former servants, including "indoor and outdoor" servants at Close House.

1

JERSEY ARCHIVE REFERENCE: D/Y/A/76/66
NOT TO BE REPRODUCED WITHOUT PERMISSION

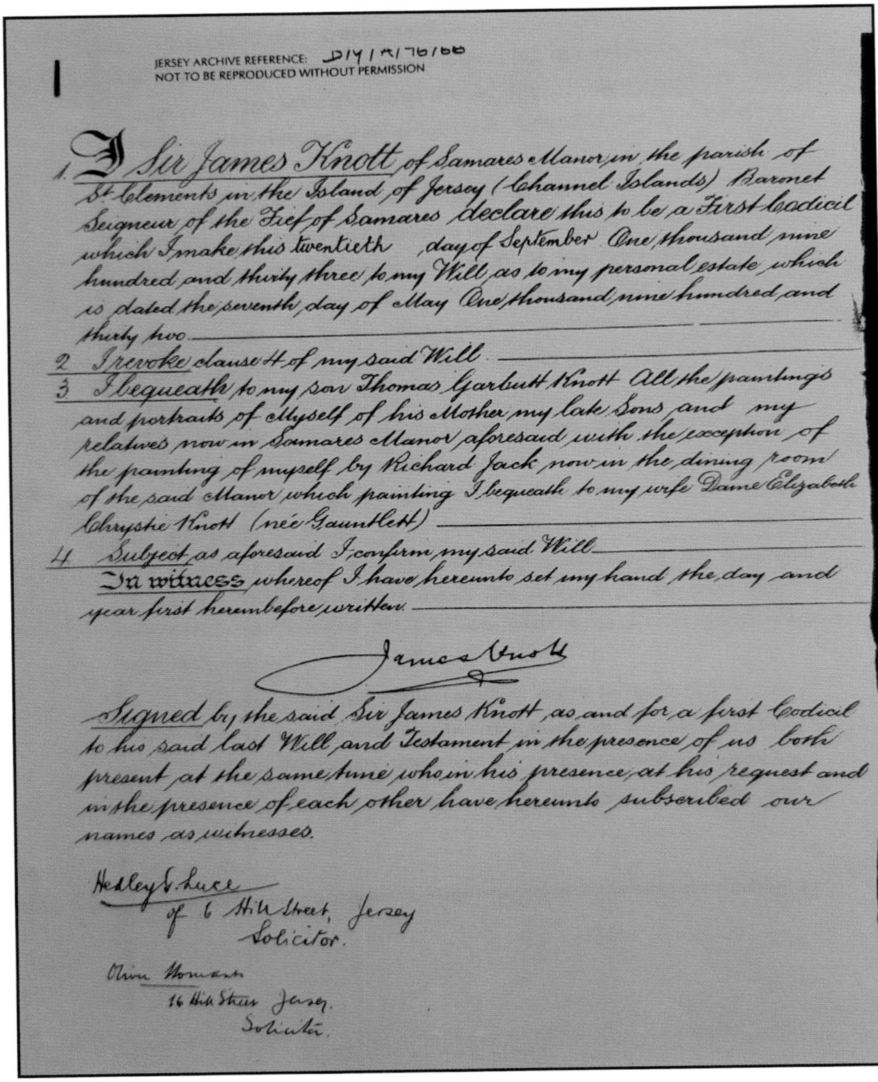

1. I Sir James Knott of Samares Manor in the parish of St Clements in the Island of Jersey (Channel Islands) Baronet Seigneur of the Fief of Samares declare this to be a First Codicil which I make this twentieth day of September One thousand nine hundred and thirty three to my Will as to my personal estate which is dated the seventh day of May One thousand nine hundred and thirty two

2. I revoke clause 4 of my said Will

3. I bequeath to my son Thomas Garbutt Knott All the paintings and portraits of Myself of his Mother my late Sons and my relatives now in Samares Manor aforesaid with the exception of the painting of myself by Richard Jack now in the dining room of the said Manor which painting I bequeath to my wife Dame Elizabeth Chrystie Knott (née Gauntlett)

4. Subject as aforesaid I confirm my said Will

In witness whereof I have hereunto set my hand the day and year first hereinbefore written

James Knott

Signed by the said Sir James Knott as and for a first Codicil to his said last Will and Testament in the presence of us both present at the same time who in his presence at his request and in the presence of each other have hereunto subscribed our names as witnesses.

Hedley G. Luce
of 6 Hill Street, Jersey
Solicitor.

Olive Norman
16 Hill Street Jersey
Solicitor.

Miss Elizabeth Chrystie Gauntlett

Miss Elizabeth Chrystie Gauntlett was the daughter of Colonel V. C. Gauntlett of the King's Regiment. She was born on 16 May 1905 in Farnham, Surrey and first met Sir James at 19 years of age when she was invited to tea at Samares Manor. She had come to Jersey with her parents when her father was stationed there in 1919 and attended the Jersey Ladies College. In early spring 1932 when she was aged 26, Sir James invited her and her French cousin Yvonne Dolfuss to join him again on the "Princess" when berthed at Monte Carlo en route for St Malo. She had previously been aboard a few times in Jersey but not on the Mediterranean. Apart from his brother Herbert, all of his ten brothers and sisters had previously died and it was said that after the death of his sons and wife of fifty years he was lonely and longed for someone he could admire and call family. Sir James was attracted by her strong character and vivacious nature, she was an accomplished horse rider, pianist and soprano having studied music and it was said she brought her own lively enthusiasm to Samares Manor. She sang and played the piano in the drawing room, entertaining Sir James and brought him happiness in the few years before he died.

Sir James proposed to Elizabeth on the bridge of Princess when en route to St Malo from Jersey and she asked for time to consider. The invited guests on board included her father, as Sir James was especially fond of him, calling him 'the old sinner'. Sir James' Jersey doctor, Dr Tom Warrington and his wife Dorothy may well have been part of the guest list. The Doctor would visit Sir James daily and take his blood pressure, only allowing him to eat his favourite steak and kidney pudding if the blood pressure was low enough. There were other friends also on board who were regularly invited, for example, for a round-the-island trip, or a trip to Sark.

The party disembarked at St Malo and travelled to Monte Carlo, via Paris, by train. Princess made the voyage there, with crew only, via the Bay of Biscay, which was considered too rough for pleasant sailing. In Paris, the party stayed at the Le Meurice Hotel, where Sir James was known and the service was good. In Paris Elizabeth consulted her cousin Yvonne, who was French by birth, on the wisdom of agreeing to Sir James' proposal. She was especially close to Yvonne partly because she was brought up as an only child and they got on really well together. Yvonne was also a good horsewoman, more serious about it than Elizabeth, later on, competing in dressage.

Elizabeth was overwhelmed by the idea of marrying Sir James Knott. She had a strong character, but was, by nature, shy and introverted. If she had to make a speech (she later became Island Commissioner of Girl Guides, then President, also President of the Commonwealth Society and British Sailors Society) it was an agonizing mountain for her to climb, but she always made it a success although it certainly didn't come naturally.

She accepted his proposal and they were married on 26 March 1932 in a civic ceremony performed at Monte Carlo by the British Consul and this was later followed on 5 April by a religious marriage ceremony in the British Embassy Church in Paris. It was reported in the press Sir James came alone to the church except for the company of his valet and smiled at his young, tall, fair haired bride as she walked up the aisle on the arm of her father, Colonel Gauntlett, who gave her away. She wore a spring like frock of champagne crepe georgette with small hat of plaited material to match, relieved with a touch of pink and blue twisted ribbons. She was attended by one bridesmaid, her cousin Yvonne Dolfuss in blue and white georgette and large picture hat. The service which was fully choral was performed by the Rev Chancellor Gordon Ponsonby, Rector of St Mary le Bow. As it was intended, the wedding should be a very quiet one, not more than a dozen people were present.

After her marriage, on her arrival at Samares, the staff were stiff and formal, finding it difficult to accept her as Sir James' new young bride. (However, after his death in 1934, she had a happy memory that all the staff, without exception, offered to stay on to serve her. It was not self-satisfaction, but she was sensitive and took some pleasure in the fact that she had convinced them of the truth, that she really cared for Sir James and had made him happy.)

Lady Elizabeth Knott

Sir James and Lady Elizabeth on their wedding April 1932

At Samares, she chose only to change the drawing room in her new home, decorating it in the William and Mary style. Sir James bought for her a Steinway piano with its case made to blend with the style of the room. Sir James was so pleased with the drawing room that he employed the same builder, W. Carpenter of Duke Street, London, to re-panel the drawing room and construct a new staircase. In the dining room prominently displayed over the fireplace is a portrait of Sir James, painted by Richard Jack who was a fashionable painter of the time. Also in the dining room is a painting also by Simon Elwes of Lady Elizabeth in her riding outfit and below her portrait sits a striking bronze of her on her favourite horse. Sir James also commissioned Richard Jack to paint a portrait of Colonel Chrystie, Elizabeth's grandfather.

To celebrate their wedding and as a gift to Elizabeth whose twenty seventh birthday was just a month away, Sir James ordered one of the new series of 20/23 Rolls Royce Phantom 2 cars with rather dashing all weather coupe coachwork. Elizabeth with Sir James' encouragement chose the design and the aluminium body was painted jade blue, Elizabeth's favourite colour and the whole colour scheme replicated that of Sir James' armorial colours, blue, sable brown and gold. Their chauffeur, Richard Ashton attended the Rolls Royce Drivers' School in London and took delivery of the car on 4 August 1932. Over the next few months they used the car frequently, travelling to the French and Italian Rivieras. Elizabeth had learned to drive but most of the time the car was driven by Ashton.

Loading the Rolls onto the Princess at Palma, Majorca

In 1932 she visited St.James' and St.Basil's Church in Fenham with Sir James and promised to return again the following year but Sir James poor health prevented this.

In 1933 Sir James donated £50,000 to the HRH Prince of Wales Fund which had been set up to provide relief to ex-servicemens dependants. He gave this in memory of his late wife and sons, to be used to provide buildings and pensions for ex-servicemen suffering from a disability.

Sir James used to cough badly, especially at night which worried Elizabeth and she obtained an invalid car for him to travel about the garden when his walking was not good enough. She was upset and hurt that she had not been present at his deathbed until after he was too ill to recognize her. Apparently, the imported nurse who was present and looking after him, didn't know who this person 'Betty' was that James was calling for.

Sir James Knott died on 8 June 1934, in Jersey after a short illness. His funeral was held at St.Clement's Church, Jersey, on 12 June, with memorial services being held at St Andrew's Parish church, in Heddon and the Church of St James and St Basil in Fenham, on the same day. Chief mourners at Jersey were Lady Knott and Sir Thomas Garbutt Knott with the crew of the yacht "Princess" lining the pathway to the church and his coffin was carried on the shoulders of six of the crew of the "Princess". His death was widely reported in the press with obituaries in the Isles of Scilly paper the Western Morning News, and the Shields News, Newcastle Journal, Sunderland Echo, Middlesbrough Gazette, Morpeth Herald, Leeds Mercury, Hull Daily Mail, Liverpool Echo, Yorkshire Post and the Belfast News. He was buried in the churchyard of St.Clement's Church, Jersey beside his first wife Margaret and on their grave is a memorial to their sons James and Basil.

 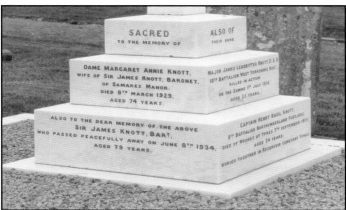

After Sir James' death, Lady Elizabeth said Samares was dismal so within weeks she set off for the continent with her Swiss maid, Berthe Egli and Richard Ashton her chauffeur. They drove across France to Lake Geneva, then across Austria, through Salzberg, Vienna to Budapest in Hungary. They returned through Italy to Venice and then north through France. Back home without Sir James' company, she was bored and planned a trip to Egypt. She had her car returned to Rolls Royce to be prepared for the trek, the engine overhauled and a luggage rack mounted on the top of the trunk to take their extra bags. Richard Ashton who was unmarried would drive and Berthe would accompany them as companion/maid and they left in November 1934.

They travelled across northern France to Paris then Monte Carlo and the Italian Riviera, crossed to Sicily and climbed Mount Etna. The next day they boarded a ship at Syracuse and sailed to Alexandria then drove to Cairo where they spent Christmas and the New Year. Lady Elizabeth had friends and contacts in Cairo and with them she explored the pyramids, lunched and partied with local princes and dignitaries, watched polo matches and rode into the desert on polo ponies where she practiced her pistol shooting and met Bedouin tribesmen. She frequently wrote to her mother and father keeping them updated about her travels and on 21 January 1935 she wrote to advise that a friend had organised a flight for her to Khartoum where she intended to stay for three days but was so enchanted with the area she sent for Berthe and Ashton to join her. They then flew to Entebee on the Equator in Uganda where they hired a car for five days to explore Uganda, where they met pygmies hunting with bows and arrows. Returning to Khartoum they stayed for a week where Lady Elizabeth enjoyed sailing races on the river, tennis and dancing at the palace of King Faisil. They then returned to Cairo where they stayed till the end of February.

In early March the car was loaded onto a pontoon and crossed the Suez then had an awful drive down the Sinai Peninsula needing once to have local Arabs get her out of deep sand. They visited Palestine, Jerusalem, Bethlehem then back to Cairo via Beersheba. On 21 March the car was shipped from Alexandria to Tangiers then they motored across Tunisia into Algeria and Morocco visiting Fez, Marrakesh and Tangiers. They crossed to Gibraltar on 10 April then drove through Spain and France and back to Jersey. Seven months later she traded in her beloved car which she had travelled in for 45,000 trouble free miles for a new Rolls Royce 25/30 series car.

Lady Elizabeth sometime after Sir James death

While she waited for the new car, she decided to go to South Africa and arrived in Cape Town on 17 March 1936. Here she took delivery of of a Ford Station Wagon and undertook another long trek through the east of Africa visiting Northern and Southern Rhodesia before departing in June from Mombasa sailing through the Suez Canal and back to Tilbury in July in time to take delivery of her new Rolls. The Natal Mercury newspaper in April reported on her journey. It recorded how she enjoyed shark fishing in False Bay and visiting the Port Elizabeth Agricultural Show where she was pleased to see Jersey Cows exhibited. Lady Elizabeth fancied another trip to North Africa and visit her friends in Cairo again so six months later with Ashton and Berthe they drove through France to the Mediterranean coast and sailed to Algeria then headed to Morocco's Atlas Mountains. A month later they returned eastwards along the Mussolini highway from Tripoli through Libya to Alexandria where they were shipped back to Syracuse arriving home by 7 May 1937.

The Sunday Grapevine, a Fleet Street newspaper printed an article in October about 1938's most amazing motoring exploit. It described Lady Knott's journeys and how she was the first Briton to drive along Mussolini's new road across Libya.

Lady Elizabeth thought it would be an ultimate adventure to cross the Sahara Desert by car and left Algiers in February 1938 in a Canadian built Ford with wide tyres and reinforced springs arriving in northern Nigeria on 14 March. They drove to Kampala, Nairobi and Mombasa from where they sailed home. Always having been impeccably dressed in his chauffeur's uniform, Richard Ashton, post-war left to nurse his sick mother while Berthe remained with Elizabeth as companion into her seventies, when she retired to live with her brother.

In 1937, in Sir James' memory, Lady Elizabeth gave to St.Andrew's Church at Heddon, pews from Newcastle Cathedral.

With the outbreak of the Second World War her travels ended and she went to London, living in Lowndes Square and worked on several committees, including the Channel Island Refugee Committee, which assisted thousands of refugees from the islands during the war. She also worked for the Motorised Transport Corps as a driver. In 1943 she married Commander Edward Owen Obbard D.S.O., G.M., R.N., who was from Jersey and known to her family, at St.Paul's Church, Knightsbridge with naval officers forming a guard of honour. After the island's liberation they returned to Jersey and had one child, Vincent, born in 1945. Edward retired from the Royal Navy in 1947 after distinguished career, having been appointed director of bomb and mine disposal at the Admiralty. Sadly,he died four years later aged just 49,so after only seven years of marriage Elizabeth was widowed again. Helped by her son she opened up the grounds of Samares to the public.

In 1958 she returned to Tyneside to attend a memorial service for Mr Rowland Lishman at Tynemouth and again on 6 June 1964 she travelled up from London on the night sleeper train to attend at Cullercoats the launching of the Sir James Knott lifeboat. This was a 37ft Oakley class lifeboat, formally named at the ceremony by Her Grace the Duchess of Northumberland and then the lifeboat was presented to the RNLI by Lady Elizabeth on behalf of the Sir James Knott Trust who had provided funding.

Then on Saturday 4 July 1998 the current owner of Lady Elizabeth's Rolls Royce, Tod Marshman and his wife Mary brought the car back to Jersey. After having had the car restored during the previous six years, after it lay for thirty years without use they had researched its history and after contacting Lady Elizabeth wanted to reunite the car with its first owner. In an article in a Rolls Royce magazine, Tod described how he met the then ninety three year old Lady Elizabeth who for the past thirty years had rarely left Samares. Although very frail and needing the constant care of a nurse he saw she still had a strong will and was a very independent character.

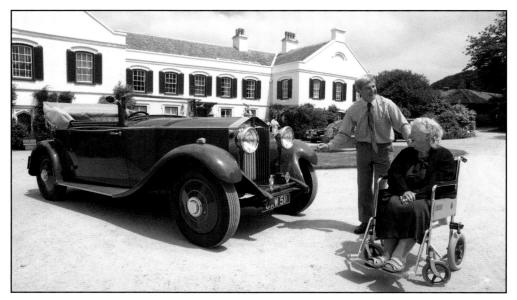

He enquired how many miles she had travelled in the car and how far and was astonished when she replied we drove 13,000 miles in thirteen weeks across Africa and Europe. He thought he misheard her as her voice was faint so asked for more details and she described all her adventures after which she had to retire for a rest. Afterwards she happily was assisted into the Rolls Royce and they went for a spin along the Jersey lanes. She loved the wind blowing through her hair again in the car which Sir James had bought for her sixty-six years previously and in which she had had so many adventures. It was said the visit and the memories it evoked filled her mind during her remaining weeks. Then having had such amazing adventures and lived for more than sixty years at Samares Manor, she died on St.Clement's Day 23 November 1998.

She is buried with her second husband in St.Clement's Churchyard just across the path from Sir James and Lady Margaret Knott. Her son, Vincent, on her death became the forty fifth Seigneur of Samares and continues to maintain the Samares Manor and grounds for public enjoyment.

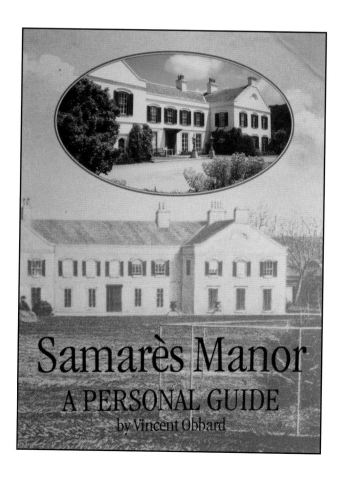

Samarès Manor
A PERSONAL GUIDE
by Vincent Obbard

10   Rowland Lishman and Knotts Flats

Rowland Lishman (1877 – 1958) was a North Shields businessman, born in Lovaine Place and later lived in Alma Place and worked in Newcastle for Pirrei, Hope and Company from January 1892. When the partnership ceased he worked for Mr Pirrei until 1896 when Pirrei was made bankrupt. He was offered a job with James Knott commencing on 2 January 1897 as invoice clerk in the chartering and export department later moving to the cash department. Two years later he was called into James Knott's office, the first time he had met him, where he was accused angrily of mishandling his position and James Knott threw his papers across the office. Next morning James Knott called him to his office explaining he had not been well and had visited his doctor who ordered a complete rest and asked him to ring the Falmouth Hotel to book him a room. A few days later he received a telegram from James Knott asking him to join him upon which he had to accompany him twice a day for a walk. He got the impression he was being examined and tested which he obviously passed as he became a lifelong friend and business confidant of James Knott.

In 1910 Prince Line shares without any apparent reason started moving up and transfers happening, so James Knott asked his chief accountant to investigate. A week later he had not got to the cause so James Knott said "you find out Rowland" upon which he got the sleeper train to London and discovered it was Sir John Ellerman of the Ellerman Shipping Company, an accountant who made a fortune buying up business, who was buying the Knott shares. He reported back to James Knott who then arranged a meeting with John Ellerman where he said he was buying Ellerman shares in retaliation and forced Ellerman to transfer back to Knott the shares in return for James Knott transferring back the Ellerman shares. His responsibilities increased rapidly after this and he represented James Knott on five boards of directors but felt his salary did not represent his position. The next year he was offered a position in the Mickley Coal Company and on advising James Knott, was offered a small rise and was told as he did work for Mrs Knott also he was regarded more as part of the family, hence his low salary. He decided to leave but was persuaded to continue on the boards of directors. Twelve months later James Knott visited him at the Mickley office and offered to double the salary Mickley paid him but he felt it unfair and refused the offer, however, he continued to be executor and trustee for Mrs Knott's affairs and he was also made executive trustee of the Knott Memorial Trust.

Rowland

The Square Building Trust was founded in 1929 by Rowland Lishman, leader of the then Northumberland Square Presbyterian Church's men's bible class after hearing a talk about the terrible housing conditions in the town. The Square Building Trust is a registered social landlord providing affordable, well-maintained homes for rent in North Tyneside.

Northumberland Square Presbyterian Church

As executive trustee of the Sir James Knott Foundation he discussed with Sir James what kind of legacy he should leave as he was nearing the end of his life.

In this letter to Rowland Lishman, Sir James proposes to build churches at Fenham and Newsham and how he would like "to do something for Shields".

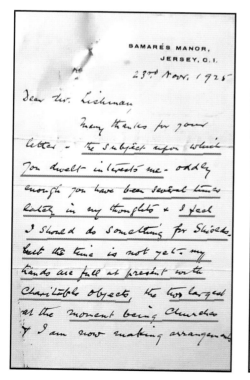

Instead of a statue, because of his interest in social housing, the development of Knotts flats was agreed as a lasting memorial to St James and after his death the trustees provided funds to build the Knott Memorial Flats and Nursery School. Miss Jean Lishman was the first superintendent of the nursery, the provision of which would have pleased the late Lady Margaret Annie Knott who all her life loved and cared for children.

Nursery School

Before the flats were constructed, the first memorial to Sir James for the benefit of the community was in 1936 with the completion of 24 three bedroomed semi-detached Douglas Haig memorial homes in Knott Place, Benwell, Newcastle. They were intended as homes for ex-servicemen with an ex-sergeant as warden and were financed by the Knott Trust.

Previously, during the Napoleonic Wars, the site of Knotts Flats had been barracks for up to 1,000 troops built in 1758. As the war ended the Square ceased to be an army barracks in 1815, the land was sold to the Duke of Northumberland and the barracks were renamed Percy Square. The Army quarters were then let as workmen's cottages and part of these cottages were still being used as living accommodation in 1925. In 1910, Tynemouth Corporation bought the land from the Duke of Northumberland for £10,000.

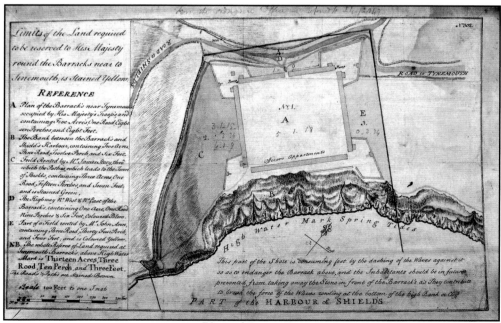

Plan of Barracks

Percy Square with the Master Mariners Home on Tynemouth Road behind.

In 1935 the Sir James Knott Housing Trust approached Tynemouth Council with plans to build 140 flats on the cliff top resulting in the square being demolished to make way for the new building. It was envisaged that the tenants selected would all be families who had some connection with the sea and already living in the North Shields district in some of the more derelict properties in the borough, scheduled for slum clearance. The architects were Tasker and Child, using local builders Stanley Miller and by 1938 they were nearing completion and the first tenants moved in in January 1939. The building boasted what was believed at the time to be the biggest clock in the North East, the timepiece was to be electrically worked and was 12ft 6in in diameter, making it easily visible from across the river in South Shields.

The original specifications said there would be three types of flats, with one, two and three bedrooms. Each flat would have a large living room, kitchenette, bathroom and a small entrance vestibule. Facilities included electric light and gas. It was said that architects had incorporated special processes to make the floors as soundproof as possible.

The flats and bankside under construction, from a magic lantern slide 1936/7

Each flat was designed to look out over the river mouth and the building would also become a notable landmark for sailors coming home to the river and that was particularly appropriate, seeing that the original intention was for some of them it would become home. Everything a modern 1938 flat should have was being incorporated. The first rents for the flats, in 1938, were 5s 10d (approx. 29p) for a one-bedroom flat; 6s 7d (approx.34p) for a two-bedroom flat; and 7s 3d (approx 36p) for a three-bedroom flat with the first tenant arriving in December of that year.

The flats newly completed.

In the Shields News dated 22 March 1935 it was reported that the Tynemouth Corporation had proposed to the Pier Committee the laying out of a public memorial park to Sir James on the Collingwood Monument field and the adjacent blockyard both of which belong to the Duke of Northumberland. It stated that since completion of the north pier the blockyard had no use and could be laid out as a public park. This was not carried out.

When the Sir James Knott Memorial Flats were officially opened, the Honourable Robert James, a director of Samares Investments Ltd made a speech about the late Sir James which was reported in the Newcastle Journal on 15 July 1937. He stated: " Sir James Knott, whom I knew very well, was extremely reticent and there was a side of him which he never revealed to anybody. There was a time when he went abroad after his two sons had been killed in the War. Some people inclined to be critical about what he had done, made certain comments. Today we realise there was no selfishness in his action in going abroad and it was not, as it was suggested to avoid taxation. The sole income from everything he possessed would ultimately be for the benefit of charities on Tyneside."

In 1948, some serious geological problems occurred when the 'toe-wall' split into two sections; the break occurring 1061ft from the west end, and causing the east section to move forward by a total of 4 feet, with a large tilting deformation becoming apparent immediately below the flats towards the centre section of the wall.

The problems were significant and urgent investigations were carried out to establish the cause of the deformations and minimise the risk of slope failure which could cause collapse of the flats, endangering the large number of families living there. It was discovered from borehole investigations, that because the toe-wall here was not grounded in rock, it had moved forward horizontally with the earth mass due to water logging of the fill material, which interrupted the natural drainage of the cliff. The toe-wall also blocked drainage by banking up the groundwater behind it. Remedial work was carried out and consisted of underpinning, reconstructing and buttressing the toe-wall, as well as draining and reshaping the cliffs to a safer profile. In April 1967 the North East Housing Association took over the management of the flats from Sir James Knott Memorial Trust. In July 2015 the flats were given a £2m facelift by the Home Group on a refurbishment programme to bring improved safety and security for the tenants. Until recently, every Christmas the elderly residents received a Christmas hamper from the trust. In 2020 the Knott Trust gave a grant to the residents committee so all residents, not just the elderly could receive a Christmas voucher.

11   Sir Thomas Garbutt Knott's later life

Thomas who bore a striking physical resemblance to his father also possessed his charitable nature. On his father's death he inherited his father's title of 2ⁿᵈ Baronet becoming Sir Thomas Garbutt Knott and £1 million but declared he had no interest in money and was known to make numerous generous anonymous gifts to worthy causes. He had a number of local friends who were authorised to bring to his attention such cases in confidence. In 1921 he had purchased Court Land estate, at Lympstone in Devon which he developed into a modern model farm employing a staff of thirteen. His father who was at that time living in Torquay made frequent visits in his steam yacht being just 12 miles along the coast. It seems after losing his two younger sons, Sir James and Thomas were reconciled and spent time in each other's company.

His globetrotting, adventurous years behind him, he now lived as a country gentleman raising Jersey cows, training his four Alsatian dogs to rescue people from fire and was a keen pigeon fancier. He was President of a number of sporting organisations in the district including the Cricket Club, Bowls Club, Snooker League, Working Men's Club and was Vice-President of Exmouth Conservative Club, Rugby Club and Swimming and Life Saving Society.

He also won many prizes for his floral entries at the Devon and Exeter horticultural shows. His principal interest however was the work of the St John Ambulance and was founder and major funder of the St.John Ambulance Association in Devon and in 1935 he gave the organisation a magnificent Austin motor ambulance which cost £850. Then garage accommodation was needed and after it was built again he went to the bank and cleared the debt. In 1936 he was made a Commander of the Hospital of St. John of Jerusalem then in 1947 he was promoted to Knight of Grace of the Order, the title which his father had borne before him. After a much needed assembly hall was built again he walked into the local bank and paid off the building debt. He was renowned for his charitable acts and in September 1934 he invited the scholars, parents and members of Lympstone Methodist Church to the grounds of his Court Land estate for an afternoon and evening of sports, races and tea. A trip to Paignton had previously been provided by Sir Thomas for the scholars of the same church. Among many other charitable acts he made was providing the village of Lympstone band with uniforms and providing a boat shelter for the fishermen. He was also a member of the "Sun" Lodge of Freemasons which gave him numerous opportunities to make other generous anonymous contributions for the welfare of distressed persons.

Then in 1936 Sir Thomas Knott gave to the village of Heddon the Knott Memorial Hall in memory of his parents and in the entrance hall is a beautiful panelled dedication with the portraits of Sir James and Lady Elizabeth. Initially the Memorial Hall was to be a more elaborate construction, the initial plans of 1935 included higher wings at the north east and south west corners to provide a news and games room at one end and a caretaker's flat at the other. In view of the relatively small size of the village, at that time, it was decided to scale down the plans and use the money saved to create an endowment fund to assist with the future upkeep of the hall. This suggestion was agreed to by Sir Thomas and his legal advisers, and the hall with Mr L.Walton-Taylor of Heddon the architect, was built by Messrs Lowry of Newcastle in 1936. The hall was requisitioned by the War Office in the period 1939-45 and was used for the billeting of troops.

Knott Memorial Hall, Heddon

After the war it was requisitioned by Northumberland County Council and after the installation of boilers and ovens it was used as a central kitchen for the provision of school meals for the surrounding area. The hall is now at the centre of the village social life, used for meetings, conferences, exercise classes, Christmas concerts, the annual village fair as well as private functions and parties.

Dedication in entrance hall.

Sir Thomas married for the second time in 1925 to his first cousin Margaret Anderson who was born in North Shields on 5 October 1883. She had previously married George Anderson who was killed in the First World War and in fact Sir James Knott was a witness at her wedding in October 1912 in Barnes, Surrey. However, soon after her marriage to Sir Thomas they separated and she lived in Exmouth with her sons from her marriage to George, where Sir Thomas continued to look after them. Margaret was four years younger than Thomas and was only sixteen years of age when Thomas went abroad in 1899 until 1919, and was married when he was away. As Thomas could hardly have known her, did Sir James suggest Thomas married Margaret to look after her after she was widowed?

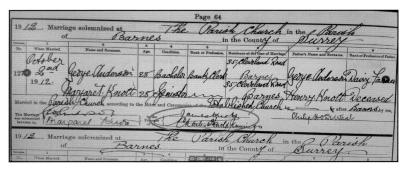

Sir Thomas had no children with Margaret and he died on 10 April 1949 aged 69 years without issue, his funeral being held at St.John's, Exmouth. At the head of the cortege was the Sir Garbutt Knott ambulance full of wreaths and flowers. For twenty eight years he had been a public benefactor to Exmouth and the local St John Ambulance Service had become one of the best equipped in the country. His estate, antique furniture and effects and farm and garden equipment were auctioned producing an estate of £56,565 from which he left £10,000 to his housekeeper and £1,000 to his chauffeur. Considering his father had left him £1 million, this shows how much he had given away to charitable causes during his life. Most of his estate was left to the Samares Investment Trust set up by his father. Margaret took little or no part in public life and died three years later on 29 November 1952 at her home 4 Merrion Avenue, Exmouth and was survived by her two sons.

From the South African Horseman in the Boer War, to a labourer in America, to a mounted trooper in the New Zealand Army and finally a gentleman farmer in Devon, he certainly had a varied colourful and adventurous life.

12   Sir James' continuing legacy

Sir James believed in 'action not words' - his many generous gifts to charities in the North East were examples of this philosophy and although there are a few records of him being a hard hearted businessman who dealt severely with those who crossed him, I believe this was not a true representation of his character as there are so many examples of his kindness to individuals throughout his life.

He was a devoted family man who was greatly affected by the death of his two youngest sons who would have succeeded him in his business interests as proved by the building and naming of the church in Fenham in their memory. When he did not get his way in renaming the church in Heddon after his sons where he had bought so much of the village, he sold all of the property there and retired away from his Tyneside roots to the Isle of Jersey.

Sir James Knott left the bulk of his £340 million estate (in today's money) to form the Sir James Knott Trust Fund. His second wife was granted an annual entitlement of £15,000, until such time as she re-married, as she did in 1943, when the sum was reduced to £10,000 per annum. A question was asked in the House of Commons, on 27 June 1934, concerning the estate of Sir James Knott, and the fact that it avoided paying death duties, as he was no longer a UK resident; however, this meant there was more money available for his charities. The Hon Robert James, a personal friend of Sir James chaired the company after Sir James's death and after he retired he was succeeded by the Duke of Northumberland, then by Viscount Ridley in 1989. Since then the chairman and trustees of the company have taken pains to follow the known wishes and preferences of Sir James in the allocation and distribution of grants to charities

In 1953 an unexpected donation was given to Salem Methodist Church, the oldest Free Church in North Shields towards alteration costs after the finding of an old baptismal register under the organ. It recorded the baptism of two brothers, Stanley and Herbert and a sister, Margaret, of Sir James Knott and when the Knott trustees were informed they sent a donation of £500 towards the work.

The trust which is responsible for making payment to registered charities was originally administered from Jersey but in 1990 the Sir James Knott Trust Settlement was divided to form the Sir James Knott Trust based in Newcastle with the reserve remaining in Jersey. The aim of the trust is to help improve the conditions of people living and working in the North East of England. Rowland Lishman as a trustee had originally proposed to Sir James the building of a new youth centre in North Shields and in 1936 the trustees bought and handed over to the trustees of the YMCA three shops at the corner of West Percy Street and Church Way as well as a generous contribution towards building costs of the James Knott Youth Centre which was completed in 1938 and today this building still provides services to the residents of North Shields. Rowland Lishman stated that the many projects completed after Sir James' death were all the things Sir James had wanted to do for the people of this area in his lifetime.

Sir James Knott YMCA in North Shields

His portrait displayed in the YMCA.

Sir James Knott's legacy extends to two of north Northumberland's most beautiful and historic estates, the College Valley Estate and Chillingham Park and its surrounding woodlands. In 1953 the College Valley Estates was purchased from the late Sir Arthur Sutherland by the Samares Investments Limited. It is regarded as one of the most beautiful and unspoilt parts of the Northumberland National Park. Then in 1982, together with the 10th Duke of Northumberland, Samares Investments Limited bought Chillingham Park to preserve the historic and unique herd of Chillingham wild white cattle. It was then managed by the Knott Trust's agents: College Valley Estates who granted a 999 year lease of the park to the Chillingham Wild Cattle Association who manage the herd.

In 2005, after a fund-raising campaign, the association purchased 330 acres of the park and surrounding woodlands so the herd and the park were reunited under the same ownership.

Sir James Knott's philanthropy is of continuing importance to the North East. Since 1990, the trust has made over 8,500 grants totalling over £27.8million, many of them to charities known to have been of keen interest to Sir James Knott including orphanages, Beamish Museum, the Old Low Light Heritage Centre, the Great North Museum, the Sage Gateshead, hospitals, universities, Shelter, Launchpad Charity providing accommodation and employment, education to servicemen in transit from military to civilian life, Citizens Advice, Bamburgh Cricket Club, disabled charities, blind homes, brass bands, housing charities, community halls, youth clubs, scouts and guides and provided a RNLI Lifeboat named Sir James Knott at Cullercoats from 1963 to 1969,

Now out of service and on display in Kirkleatham Museum.

In 2021, the Sir James Knott Trust pledged to make £2 million worth of grants from the Newcastle branch and £1.5 million from the Jersey branch and has managed assets worth over £130million. It continues to make charitable grants, a remarkable legacy for this North Shields gentleman whose wealth achieved by his entrepreneurial ventures, continuing to benefit the lives of people throughout the region.

So apart from being a philanthropist, student, ship-owner, barrister, Member of Parliament, churchman, sportsman, yachtsman, farmer and gardener he was a loving family man and one of the merchant giants of the 19th century. His life and philanthropy has certainly benefited and improved the lives of so many people in so many different ways, an amazing legacy I think you must agree.

Yet to think how easily none of this legacy could have existed.

If Sir James' father in law hadn't died so young resulting in his family moving to North Shields enabling James to meet his daughter Margaret, then Sir James being involved in the teetotal movement of the Methodist Church resulting in rather than going into his father's wine business, going into the shipping business and being such a successful businessman, the Sir James Knott Trust would have not existed.

Then we would not be talking about this generous philanthropic Tyneside gentleman who despite his later luxurious life never forgot his North Shields roots.

Acknowledgements

The author wishes to express his sincere thanks for the invaluable assistance and information from the following sources:-

Jo Curry MBE, DL, of the Sir James Knott Trust for the pictures of Sir James, Thomas, Henry , James, Lady Margaret, the yacht "Princess" and the brig "Pearl".

YMCA North Shields for the portrait of Sir James Knott.

Vincent Obbard at Samares Manor, Jersey for the pictures of Samares Manor, Lady Elizabeth and her wedding photograph and so much information about his mother, Lady Elizabeth.

North Shields Library Local Studies Department.

John Wraith HappyChappyImages, for the cover picture of the Mouth of the River Tyne.

Jersey Evening Post Collection at Jersey Archive for the picture of Lady Elizabeth Knott in 1998.

Yorkshire Film Archive for the picture of Sir James and Lady Elizabeth on board Princess and her Rolls Royce being loaded on board.

Ian Ronayne, Jersey author/historian, for information about Sir James' time at Jersey.

The Rev. James McGowan, of the St James and St Basil Church, Fenham.

Frank Taylor and the Royal National Lifeboat Institution archives for the pictures and information of the Sir James Knott lifeboat.

Rachel Chapman from the Old Low Light Heritage Centre, North Shields for reading and editing my numerous drafts of this book.

Mike N Coates

References:

A History of the Knott Family   by   Joan R Duckett

Pride of the Princess   by   Norman L Middlemiss

Newcastle Shipowner   by   John Dobson

Cullercoats Lifeboats   by   Nicholas Leach

Local Studies Section of North Shields Library

Heddon on the Wall   History Society website

British Newspaper Archive website

Yorkshire Film Archive

.

printed by   printnortheast